INTERNATIONAL
Textile Design

INTERNATIONAL
Textile Design

Mary Schoeser

Assistant Editor Jennifer Hudson

Laurence King

In memory of *Eddie Squires* (1940–1995), former Design Director at Warner Fabrics.

19508
————
7146

Published 1995 by
Laurence King Publishing

Copyright © 1995
Calmann & King Ltd

A catalogue record for
this book is available
from the British Library.

ISBN 1 85669 072 5

Designed by Lee Bullett
and Richard Smith
at Area, London

Printed in Hong Kong

(Frontispiece)
Clare Goddard
Tea Shells
Constructed fabric
One-off
Rubber-coated, split
used tea bags, thread
Piece width
50cm (19⅝in)
Piece length
300cm (118in)

Acknowledgements

From around the world,
textile designers and
makers submitted a total
of some 1,150 images
from which the selection
of about 250 was made.
Those with selected
work are listed in the
biographies. Those who
could not be included
are, unfortunately, too
numerous to mention,
but I would like to thank
them all equally; it was
both a pleasure and
privilege to choose from
such a rich and varied
group of textiles. I am
also indebted to Montse
Stanley, Janet de Boer
and Joanna Mandl Inc.
who encouraged
submissions from
designers in Spain,
Australia and Italy
respectively; to the
designers of the book,
Richard Smith and
Lee Bullett at Area; and
to the team at Calmann
& King, particularly
Laurence King, Joanne
Lightfoot and Jennifer
Hudson. Finally, for
offering both advice and
enthusiastic support in
the formative stages of
this project, I would like
to express my gratitude
to Charles Metcalfe,
Chairman of the Design
and Product Marketing
Division of the Textile
Institute.

Mary Schoeser

Contents

1. **Koji Hamai**
14 1/2 – 4 (detail)
Installation June 1994
300 Cotton T-shirts
displayed in a space
of 228m (750ft)

● New Directions

2. (Top) **Teresa Pla**
Sphere
Five-layered sprang
construction
One-off
Cotton
Width
45cm (17⅞in)
Height
45cm (17⅞in)

3. (Above) **Developed
by Courtaulds Fibres**
Tencel Fibre
100 per cent
cellulosic
fibre made from
wood pulp. Used
by over 100 fabric
manufacturers
worldwide

Textiles today encompass a wide range of effects, techniques and ingredients that at first glance seem very disparate: new fibres, fabric treatments or computer technology often provide a starting point; so too do long-established practices and the natural fibres from which all textiles were made prior to the twentieth century. Yet this diversity is underpinned by a network of shared interests in detail, whether expressed as surface texture alone, subtle pattern and shading, or choices based on the physical and chemical nature of individual elements that make up the total. In this context 'detail' does not mean fussiness, but instead places the desire for integrity at the heart of all of the questions now being asked about fibre creation and processing, dyeing, weaving, printing and designing. Reflecting this trend, the selection criteria for this, the first volume of **International Textile Design**, placed integrity of concept and construction before novelty; some makers and designers are well-known, others are reaching an international forum for the first time. Over thirty countries are represented, demonstrating the variety of ways in which respect for the essence of textiles – both as fabric and as an expressive medium – underpins the work of the innovative designers, manufacturers and makers around the world.

This volume also reflects the significance of the growing recognition that industry and craftspeople have much to offer each other; it can be argued that they always did, but the creation of opportunities for shared,

interactive innovation has only become possible with the arrival of the third industrial revolution, based on computer and information technology. The installation of computer-aided design and manufacturing systems represents a departure from the linear progression of the first and second industrial revolutions, which initially gave us mass production and then, in the years between 1945 and 1985, much higher speeds and standards but greater uniformity. Recent developments have reintroduced flexibility by eliminating the bottlenecks formerly created by the design proofing, or sampling, and machine set-up stages; designs generated by computer-aided design (CAD) systems can also be sold prior to production, and can be used to create colour separations and drive laser engravers. In addition, this new technology facilitates exploration without restricting methods of production. Just some of the possibilities are represented by the collaborations of Margot Rolf and Anne Hübel with ZSK, producing seemingly one-of-a-kind embroideries on computer-controlled machines; the hand weaves of Jorun Schumann, who develops doubleweave designs on computer; Dorte Østergaard Jakobsen's use of a computer to digitize photographs for silk-screen printing; and Diann Parrott's hand-printed allusions to repeat created with a combination of computer-generated photostencils, repetitive body movements and string-grid systems. The boundaries between low and high technologies have seldom been so blurred.

5. (Right) **Reiko Sudo**
Slipstream
Jacquard weave
Silk, paper
Piece width
110cm (43in)
Repeat length
3.5cm (1⅜in)
Manufacturer: Nuno
Corporation, Japan

4. **Du Pont de Nemours
International SA**
*Nomex III Safety
Garments*
95 per cent
meta-aramid fibre,
5 per cent Kevlar fibre
Made to measure
Manufacturer: Du
Pont de Nemours
International SA,
Switzerland

There are other indications that barriers have come down. The rapid response required by mainstream fashion houses (which absorb close to half of all manufactured textiles) was the crucial factor behind the first installations of quick, flexible computer aids. This in turn has supported an even greater pace of fashion change (expressed to a large extent through varying the handle, weight and character of the cloth) as well as the desire for less than gigantic production runs. Many textile designers now use working methods that suit both one-off or medium-output production so that fabrics once exclusive to couture collections are more widely accessible. In the past closely associated with the Japanese textile designer Junichi Arai and his Nuno Corporation (which continues to evoke the aesthetics of hand-crafted cloths through innovative manipulation of both ancient and new fibres and technologies), this is now a widespread concept. In Slovenia, for example, Almira Sadar and Marija Jenko work polyester fibre into high-relief felt, shaped by hand or industrial production processes.

The blurred line between scales of manufacturing is paralleled by a lack of distinction between fashion and furnishing fabrics; for designers such as Koji Hamai, the concept is 'fabric' rather than 'function'. For others, such as Romeo Gigli, the concept resides in a particular quality; in the case of 'Theodora', which was created first as a gauzy shirting, it was the intriguing subtlety of the design that, with the help of the Donghia Design Studio

and mill, was transferred to an upholstery-weight silk and linen cloth. Because concepts so often take precedence, attempting to differentiate between functional and contemplative textiles can be misleading. Isabella Whitworth, for example, produces painted silk scarves that are often also used as wall-hangings, no doubt because she does not see herself as a textile designer, but rather as a painter who, responding to the ideas being explored, chooses the correct surface – sometimes cloth, sometimes paper. New attitudes have extended the manipulation of paper itself; its cellulosic structure makes it flexible, and it can be recycled with fabric, as in Karen Smith's work, or used alone, as in Grethe Wittrock's pleated kimono. Reiko Sudo, principal designer at Nuno, uses paper to demonstrate another way in which fashion and interiors collide; her 'Slipstream' cloth combines silk organdy with handmade Mino paper, a *kozo* paper widely used for translucent sliding doors in Japanese homes today.

Many materials originally designed for industrial purposes are also broadening the horizons of designers. Jan Truman has developed a technique for knitting wire which allows her to explore structure, movement and light in ways not possible with conventional yarns, and she often juxtaposes small electrical components with gems to introduce a quirky 'realism' into her 'idealized' structures. Luis Omar Acosta, on the other hand, uses a tough

but semi-sheer non-woven fabric (more familiar in their cleaning cloth and hospital gown guise) as a basis for 'Transparent Symphony'. Glass, polyamide, elastane, aramid, carbon and metalized fibres now bind together the science and art of textiles; Courtaulds' aluminized rayon (Novus®), Du Pont's meta-aramid fibre (Nomex®) and Agripac's polypropyline strain-indicating bands offer some evidence of a form of innovative design that is largely invisible to the consumer but is nevertheless stimulating new ideas about fabric behaviour and construction.

The implications of environmental and ecological issues have created ideological links between many different types of textiles. Yarns, fabrics and fashions composed of recycled materials are increasingly marketed as such, and in most cases ecological concerns are foremost. But for others such as Heather Allen, the motivation could be described as spiritual; she recycles the discarded clothing and textiles of those around her into rag rugs, *because* they are laden with nuances that illuminate the intimacy cloth shares with daily life. For centuries both types of recycling have been intrinsic to textile making: the spiritual in rugs, quilting and appliqué, the practical in cloths such as shoddy (made from recarded and spun wool) and yarns such as filloselle (spun silk waste). New methods of utilizing textile waste are the subject of investigation around the world – Hamai uses waste yarn, Clare Goddard uses teabags – while the

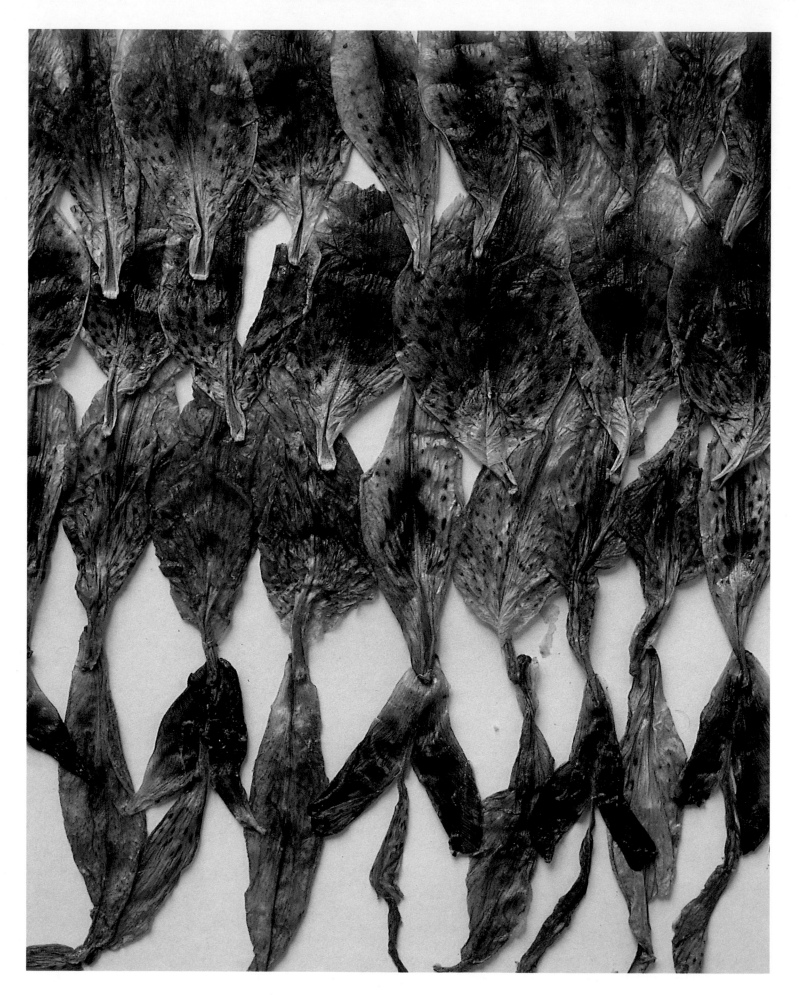

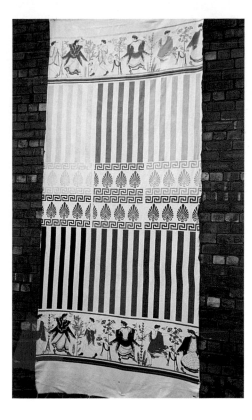

6. (Far left)
Clare Goddard
Preservation
Constructed fabric
One-off
Flower petals,
industrial coating
used for preservation
Piece width
50cm (19⅝in)
Piece length
50cm (19⅝in)

7. (Left)
Diana von Cranach
Savants II
Dobby woven, block-
printed and hand
screen-printed aqueous
finished fabric
Linen warp, cotton weft
(Nantes quality)
Piece width
152.4cm (60in)
Manufacturer: Glenanne
Prints, UK

8. **Toray Industries Inc.**
Escaine Microfabrics
Synthetic suede
formed from bunches
of ultra-microfibres
(polyester, polymer)
Fashion design:
Sybilla, Spain
Manufacturer: Toray
Industries Inc, Japan

containment of waste from production processes was the challenge met by Courtaulds' recently launched Tencel®, a cellulose-based fibre made by a fully recycling, no-effluent system. The basis for this lyocell fibre (the generic term agreed in 1989) is far more 'green' than cotton; Courtaulds Fibres are using eucalyptus grown on marginal land, with each crop harvest leaving five per cent of the trees uncut. However, the end result is a sophisticated fibre that through fibulation can produce peach skin- and suede-like cloths. The advent of suede-like fabrics dates from 1970 and the introduction of Escaine© by Toray using a spinning technique invented by Miyoshi Okamoto while meditating on a whirlpool. Constantly improved, fabrics made from this polyester ultra-microfibre (far finer than human hair) now provide an alternative to leather that not only acknowledges animal-rights campaigns, but is actually superior to suede in its colour fastness, weather resistance and washability.

Equally subtle is the use of restraint as an ecological principle; Irene Paskvalic's weaves demonstrate how effective cloth construction and natural fibre colours are in place of added colour. The less commonly used natural fibres, such as jute, canabis, ramie, horsehair and Colombian cajatropis, also provide positive alternatives. The choice of imagery can provide a far more evident expression of concern for the environment, and a noticeable feature of fabrics from

around the world is their depiction of endangered species and cultures. The preservation of a culture is closely allied to the preservation of its craft skills, and this has extended the appreciation of many old techniques, which can not only recreate ancient (or document) fabrics and contribute to the maintenance of a way of life, but also produce beguilingly simple textiles that express the essence of cloth. The conjunction of an interest in folklore or mythology with old textile techniques can be found in innovative work as diverse as that of the Maki sisters, whose handwoven cloths are woven exclusively for them in the Indian workshop run by the designer Neeru Kumar, and that of Tilleke Schwarz, whose embroidered panels incorporate elements, such as stitched laundry marks, once practiced by countless sampler makers. These designers maintain their integrity by responding to the past rather than copying it; others do so by drawing upon their personal past, upon reflections of their own inner world, a theme strong enough to warrant its own chapter. Still more – Carolyn Quartermaine, for example – are inspired by ancient images, rather than techniques, although many of the document fabrics combine both. Diana von Cranach, whose 'Savants II Collection' explores motifs from Greek and Etruscan pottery and architecture, works with craftswomen in India, Egypt and the East to create what she calls 'usable, wearable, recyclable cloth; if you don't like it any more, you can carry your potatoes in it.' Her statement reflects the themes that run

as an undercurrent through the works, all from 1993 and 1994, illustrated in this volume: worldwide connections, shared concerns, and the new-found flexibility of old and new technology working in tandem, all providing springboards for innovation with integrity.

1. (Left)
**Christopher Leitch/
Stephanie Sabato**
Autumn/Plum Dynasty
Hand-dyed window
treatments
One-off
Japanese silk habutai/
spun Chinese silk,
moulds
Piece width
114.3cm (45in)
Manufacturer:
Ganga, USA

Section

① **The Natural World**

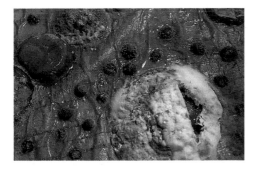

2. (Above)
**Christopher Leitch/
Stephanie Sabato**
*Oranges, Melons
and Grapes*
Hand-dyed fabric
One-off
Wild silk, handspun
and woven in India
Detail view during
pattern cultivation
process
Manufacturer:
Ganga, USA

Nature has long been a source of inspiration for textile designers, but images of nature – and natural fibres themselves – now carry political and philosophical significance that designers and makers choose to confront directly or obliquely, taking a wide view or being highly specific or, just to complicate matters, using natural fibres or images of nature simply because they are the best solution to the task at hand. Whatever the motivation, the emphasis is on the wild, on its fragility, beauty and value.

Among the images of the natural world are those declaring support for well-recognized principles, including the protection of endangered species; this inspired Margara Griffin's imagery. But the depiction of animals on fabrics can also contain a sense of fun; normally associated with designs for children, animals – the more exotic the better – have invaded grown-up textiles. Images may acknowledge the right to cultural differences; this lies behind the forms chosen by Vallerie Maden to represent the imposition of Western standards on the Third World, as well as the photographic images that make up Razia Ahmed's patchwork panel. Annette Nix's carpets incorporate objects reflecting different aspects of life that have been exploited or destroyed by the Western World.

The fragility of nature is subtly conveyed by imagery focused on transience: Dorte Østergaard Jakobsen begins by photographing wind turbulence patterns in sand, while Anne Morrell's embroideries evolve as she observes the juxtaposed tension and harmony of her pond's surface. Stojanka Strugar's tapestries evoke the powerful but unpredictable movement of the living world, in which 'nature and human beings are wrenched out of their true nature'.

The life cycle itself inspired Koji Hamai's creation of one hundred bodies from old cloths and rags, for an installation which describes 'all the substances surrounding the human body that deteriorate and then revive'. Ganga, or Stephanie Nuria Sabato and Christopher Leitch, address the same dynamic through the use of yeast, moulds and other fungi cultivated on cloth surfaces to develop pattern and colour, eschewing toxic synthetic dyestuffs and treatment chemicals in favour of living matter.

An emphasis on ecologically sound materials is reflected throughout this volume, but in relation to the natural world, Kirsten Nissen and Anne Fabricius Møller's use of willow suggests the value of well-managed, copiced woodlands. Broader ethical management   of all aspects of design and production – is exemplified by Esprit's Ecollection: the use of low-impact dyes, organic cottons, recycled wools and chemical-free finishing processes are just some of the end results of their evaluation of the social and environmental impact of their clothing, and the firm also eco-audits their staff's working environment.

6. (Right)
**Christopher Leitch/
Stephanie Sabato**
Flowers/Haricot Verts
Hand-dyed
blouse/waistcoat
One-off
Japanese silk broad-
cloth, moulds
Manufacturer:
Ganga, USA

3. **Margara Griffin**
Looking Forward
Hand-dyed and
hand screen-
printed fabric
Prototype
Cotton, aniline
dye, pigments

4. **Jane Poulton**
And Then What
Machine-sewn
embroidery
One-off
Mercerized cotton
thread, linen
ground cloth
Height
21.5cm (8½in)
Length
17cm (6⅝in)

5. (Right)
G. P. & J. Baker
*Wadi Halfa (from Baker
Company seal c. 1894)*
Jacquard chenille weave
51 per cent modacrylic,
48 per cent viscose,
1 per cent polypropylene
Piece width
140cm (55in)
Width repeat
35cm (13¾in)
Length repeat
34cm (13⅜in)
Manufacturer: G.P. &
J. Baker Ltd, UK

8. **Lena Cronholm**
Cayenne, Pampas,
Eternell
Machine screen prints
Cotton
Width repeat 23cm
(9in); 150cm (59in);
15cm (5⅞in)
Length repeat 30cm
(11¾in); 79cm (31in);
15cm (5⅞in)
Manufacturer: Borås
Cotton AB, Sweden

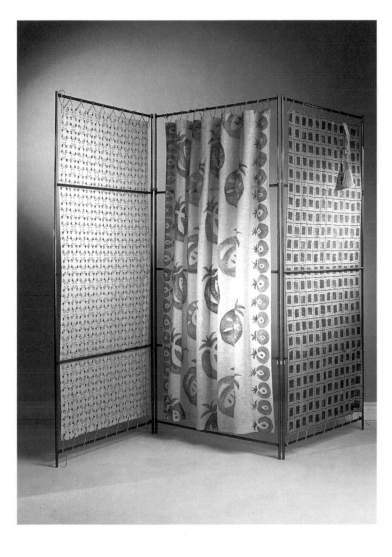

9. **Françoise Dorget**
Untitled (Essential
Collection)
Screen print
Plain woven cotton
Piece width
143cm (56¼in)
Manufacturer:
Fujie Textile Co.
Ltd, Japan

7. (Left) **Sanderson**
Compassionate Leaves
Doublecloth weave
with appliqued effect
Cotton
Piece width
137cm (53⅞in)
Length repeat
32cm (12½in)
Manufacturer:
Sanderson, UK

10. **Jilly Edwards**
Solitaire
Tapestry
One-off
Cotton warp; wool,
chenille, linen weft
Width
90cm (35⅜in)
Height
70cm (27½in)

11. (Right)
Isabella Whitworth
Leaf and Lizard Shawl
Resist dyed and hand-
stitched
One-off
Silk mousseline,
Kniazeff dyes, beads,
paints
Width 100cm (39⅜in)
Height 200cm (78⅜in)

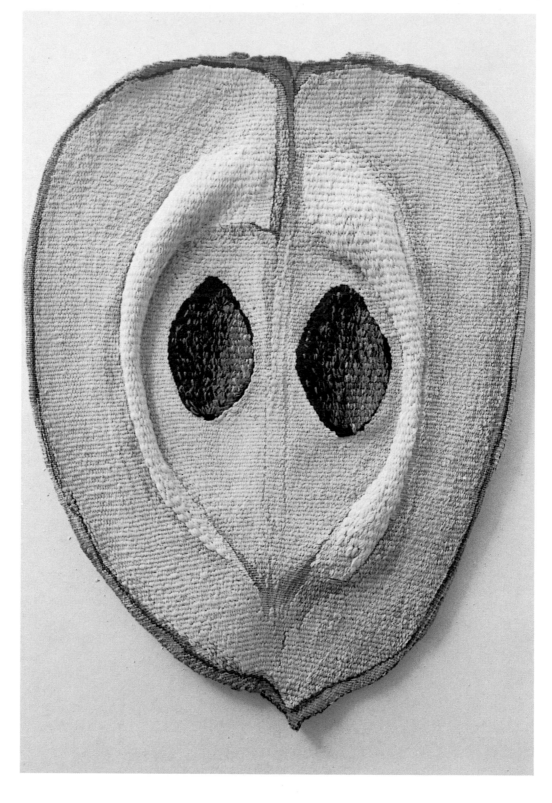

12. **Christianna Los**
Fruit Form II
Tapestry
One-off
Hand-dyed
silk and wool
Width
78cm (30⅝in)
Height
106cm (41⅝in)

13. **Christianna Los**
Fruit Form III
Tapestry
One-off
Hand-dyed wool
Width
80cm (31⅝in)
Height
93cm (36½in)

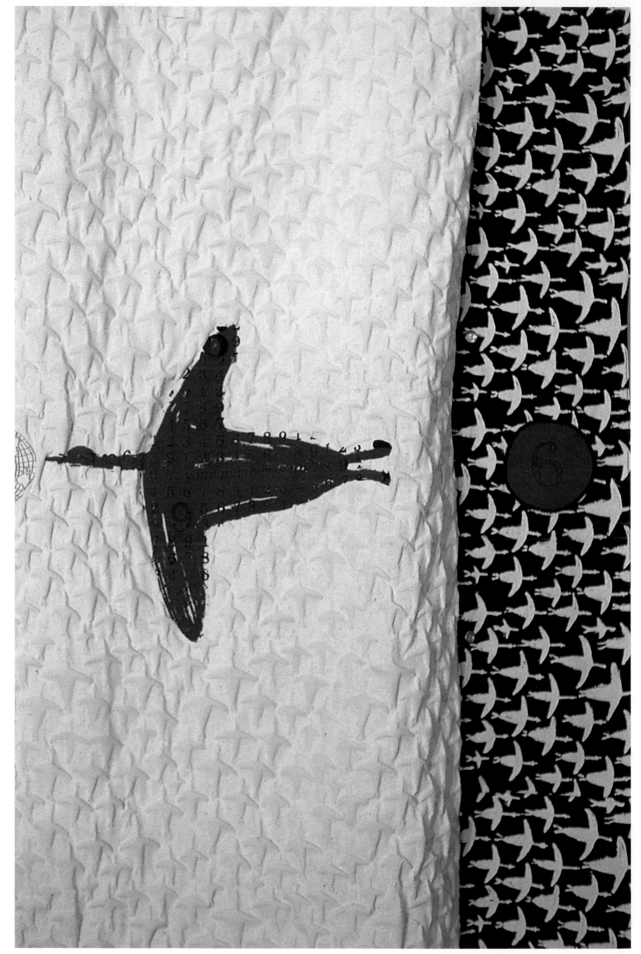

14. **Patrick Snelling**
Numbers Game
Machine-stitched,
hand screen print
Limited batch
production
Cotton, silk,
pigmented heat-
sensitive inks
Piece width
196cm (77⅛in)
Piece length
126cm (49½in)

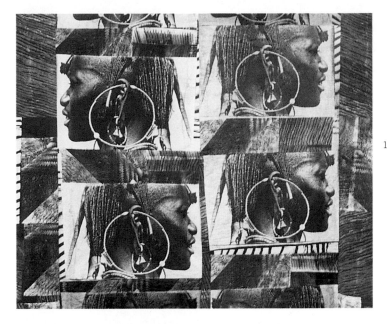

15. **Razia Ahmed**
Untitled
Vandyke brown
printed, machine-
stitched patchwork
wall-hanging
One-off
Unginned cotton
cloth
Width
147cm (58in)
Height
248.9cm (98in)

16. **Maarten Vrolijk**
Zoo 2
Handtufted rug
Limited batch
production
Pure new wool
Width
200cm (78⅜in)
Height
200cm (78⅜in)
Manufacturer:
Maarten Vrolijk
Editions, The
Netherlands

17. **Liza Collins**
Planting Ground
Tapestry
One-off
Cotton warp;
hand-dyed wool,
cotton, rayon weft
Width
104cm (40⅞in)
Height
80cm (31½in)

18. **Annette Nix**
Emptiness
Handtufted rug
One-off
Wool, glass, stone
Width
150cm (59in)
Height
600cm (236⅛in)

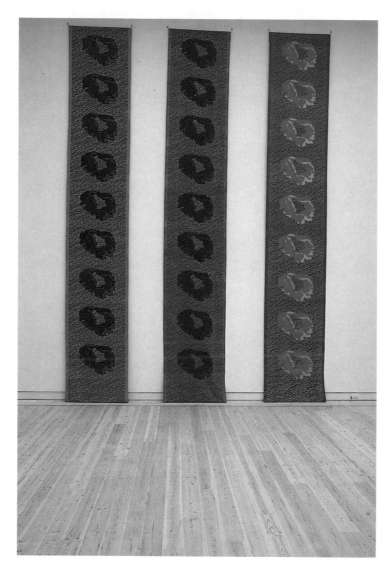

20. (Right) **Dorte Østergaard Jakobsen**
Sand
Direct silkscreen print
Prototype
Linen
Piece width
140cm (55in)
Piece length
700cm (275½in)
Width repeat
31cm (12⅛in)
Length repeat
27cm (10⅝in)

19. **Dorte Østergaard Jakobsen**
Flower on the Sand
Direct and discharge silkscreen print
Prototype
Linen, cotton
Piece width
110cm (43¼in)
Piece length
700cm (275½in)
Width repeat
100cm (39⅜in)
Length repeat
75cm (29½in)

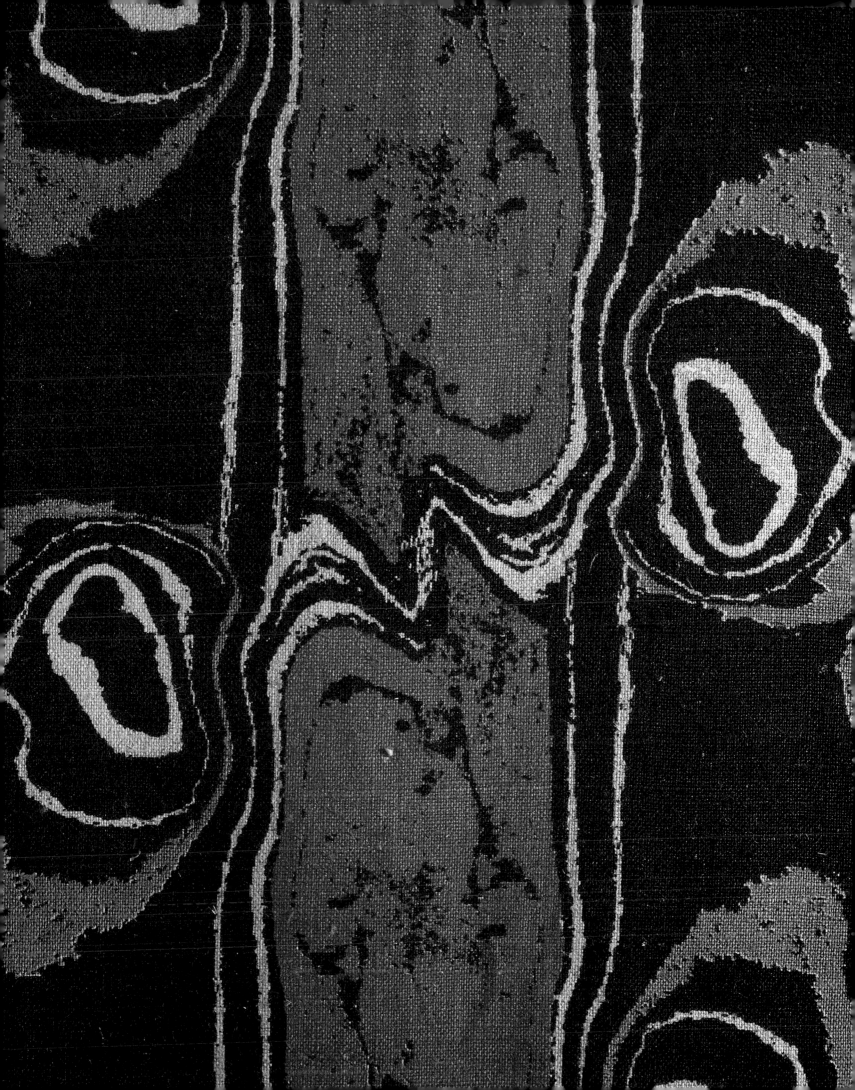

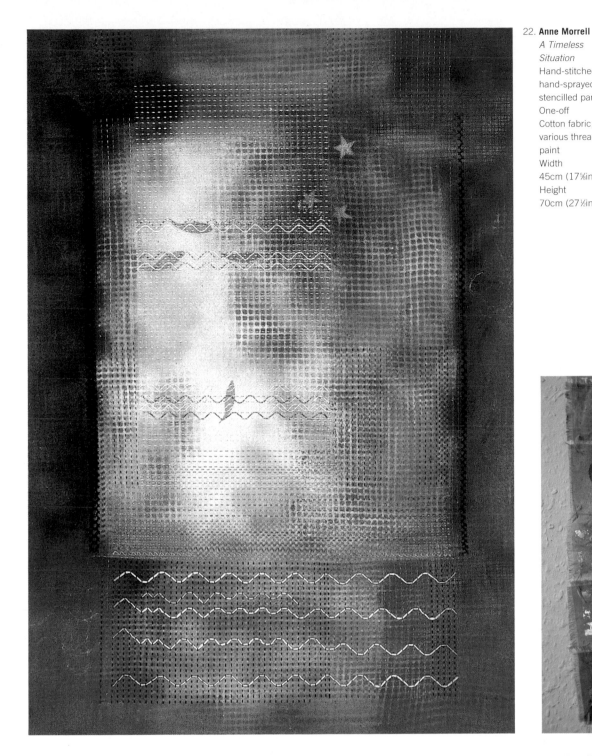

22. Anne Morrell
*A Timeless
Situation*
Hand-stitched,
hand-sprayed,
stencilled panel
One-off
Cotton fabric,
various threads,
paint
Width
45cm (17⅝in)
Height
70cm (27½in)

23. Anne Crowther
Untitled
Constructed textile
One-off
Naturally dyed
and distressed
cotton, appliquéd
metal leaf, leaves
Width
30cm (11¾in)
Height
80cm (31½in)

21. (Left) **Reiko Sudo**
Scrapyard
Hand-printed cloth
Limited batch
production
Rayon, rust
Piece width
53cm (20⅞in)
Piece length
160cm (63in)
Manufacturer:
Hiroko Kobayashi/
Nuno Laboratory,
Japan

24. **Anne Morrell**
*Inhabiting
Worlds*
Hand-stitched,
hand-sprayed,
stencilled panel
One-off
Cotton fabric,
various threads,
paint
Width
57cm (22⅜in)
Height
46cm (18in)

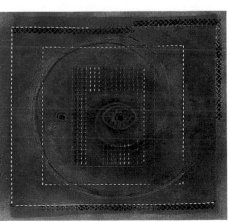

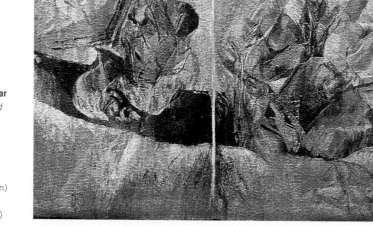

25. **Stojanka Strugar**
   Thinking Aloud
   in Orange
   Tapestry
   One-off
   Sisal, tow
   Width
   400cm (157⅜in)
   Height
   200cm (78⅜in)

26. **Stojanka Strugar**
   Three Figures
   Tapestry
   One-off
   Wool
   Width
   160cm (63in)
   Height
   180cm (70⅞in)

27. **Keiko Amenomori
Schmeisser**
*Red-black
Mountain*
Hand screen-
printed fabric
Cotton
Piece width
87cm (34¼in)
Length repeat
65cm (25½in)

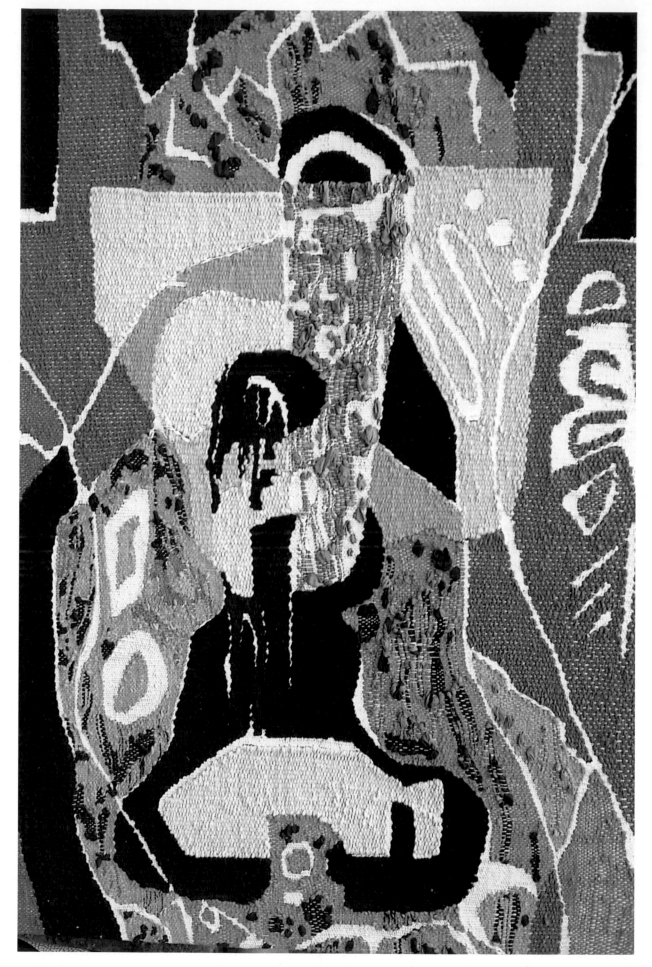

28. **Kristine Birzniece**
Composition
Tapestry
One-off
Wool, flax, capron
Width
100cm (39⅜in)
Height
135cm (53⅛in)
Manufacturer:
Latvian Art
Academy

29. **Vallerie Maden**
Back to the Future
Embossed, collaged and appliqued hand-made paper with machine and hand stitching
One-off
Paper, silk chiffon, copper sheet, wire purls
Width
80cm (31½in)
Height
55.9cm (22in)

30. **Koji Hamai**
When a woman dies in anything but murder she turns sideways
(detail)
Installation 1994
One-off
One hundred bodies made of old clothes and rags hang in an ammonite-shaped spiral

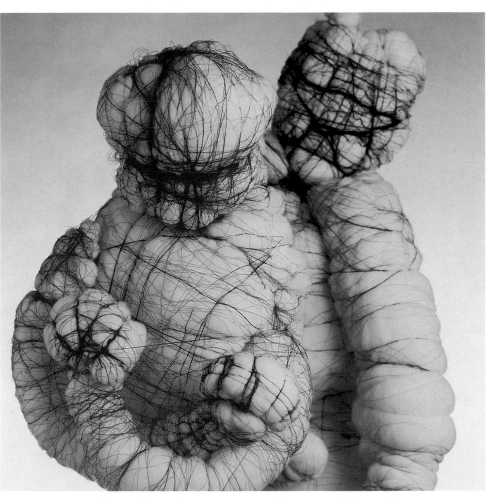

31. (Right & far right) **Sally Fox**
Fox Fiber
Handloomed knit
88 per cent Fox Fiber, 12 per cent unbleached/ undyed conventional cotton yarn
One size only
Manufacturer: Esprit, USA

The current fashion for 'natural look' textiles often collides with the environmental issues surrounding cotton, the fibre that accounts for the greatest proportion of natural fibre production. Alone among the natural fibres, cotton production increased significantly during the twentieth century, but only through increasingly intense applications of pesticides; the dyeing of cotton, particularly with synthetic indigo, also creates damaging waste. **Sally Fox**, an American agricultural scientist and farmer, has confronted both problems by growing cotton crops mulched in natural colouring fertilizers. In conjunction with Levi Jeans, she has created 'green' jeans, and her own range of eco-cloth is marketed as *Fox Fiber* and is used by, among others, Esprit.

31. (Right)
Kirsten Nissen
*Travelling Rug
for a Giraffe*
Handwoven rug
in a skip-tabby
technique
Prototype
Worsted, wool
Width
110cm (43¼in)
Height
200cm (78⅜in)

32. **Anne Fabricius
Møller** in
collaboration with
Niels Hvass
Willow Chair
Stacking chair
Limited batch
production
Willow and iron
Width
70cm (27in)
Height
95cm (37⅜in)

33. **Kirsten Nissen**
Twiggy
Handwoven
upholstery fabric
Limited batch
production
Trevira warp;
willow twig weft
Chair designed
by Niels Hvass
Manufacturer:
Octo, Denmark

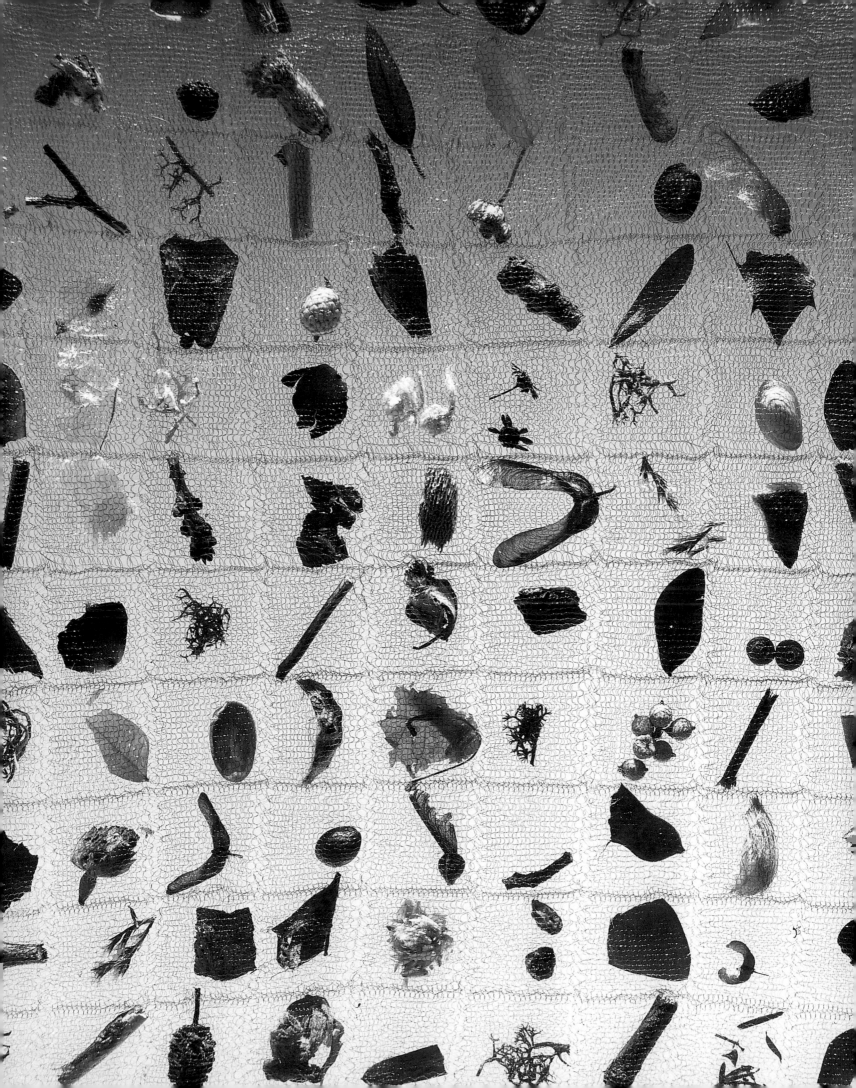

1. (Left) **Susie Freeman**
Fallen Fragments
Machine-knit
with 'pockets'
enclosing objects
Limited batch
production
Nylon monofilament
yarn, leaves, seeds,
pods, berries, wood
Piece width
76.2cm (30in)
Piece length
46cm (18in)

Section

(2) ● # Light &
Shade

2. (Above) **Susie Freeman**
Neck cowl
Machine-knit
with 'pockets'
enclosing objects
Limited batch
production
Nylon monofil-
ament, shells,
polished stones
Piece width
38cm (15in)
Piece length
20.3cm (8in)

Of all the raw materials used in the creation of fine and decorative arts, textiles are unique in offering the potential for juxtaposed densities as an integral part of their structure. The evident appreciation of the unique aesthetics of new and improved synthetics has combined with much of the exploration of this essential characteristic, to produce a degree of investigation of light and shade not seen since the 1920s and '30s.

The weaver and knitter manipulate spaces as well as yarns; the fewer yarns there are in a given area, the more transparent it becomes. However simple this principle seems, it can provide a complex interplay of light and shade, particularly when combined with materials that are themselves reflective or translucent. Susie Freeman continues to delight with her machine-knitted pocketcloths, ensnaring shiny objects in a gauzy web. Creating her networks by weaving, Zoe Hope incorporates both natural and man-made finds, including watch parts. Marie-Louise Rosholm, in contrast, has designed a woven curtain fabric for Fede Cheti that prompts a play of light across twisted cotton wefts. Gary Rooney heat treats blister-knit jersey fabrics to enhance the sheen of lurex and calendered scales. For Sahco Hesslein, Ulf Moritz explores the potential of polyester.

Because textiles also provide a surface, degrees of opacity can be created by a diverse range of printing techniques. Pat

Hodson uses wax resist in layers to push dye saturations to their limit while retaining the purity and transparency of colour. Ray Pierotti uses a unique method of direct dyeing to create subtle luminescent streaks; direct dyeing is also Diann Parrott's method, but her use of transparent textile inks results in textural marks that capture the spontaneity of hand printing. Handpainting and resist combine in Iben Brøndum's reversible translucent cloths, while Robert Lamarre produces prints inspired directly by the play of light and shadow.

Devoré – revived for fashion by Galliano in the late 1980s but new to furnishings in the mid-1990s – and Junichi Arai's 'melt-off' are also print processes, subtracting velvet and lamé respectively, leaving a ground which was impervious to the printed heat-reactive reductive paste. And among the ethereal textures are floating wefts, slit and left to dance or clipped back to create shadowy outlines, giving both texture and translucence to the work of Ulf Moritz and Irene Paskvalic.

3. **Wei Zhu**
   The space (detail)
   Construction
   One-off
   Palm, metal wire,
   cotton band
   Width 66cm
   (25⅞in)
   Height 105cm
   (41⅓in)
   Depth 70cm
   (27½in)

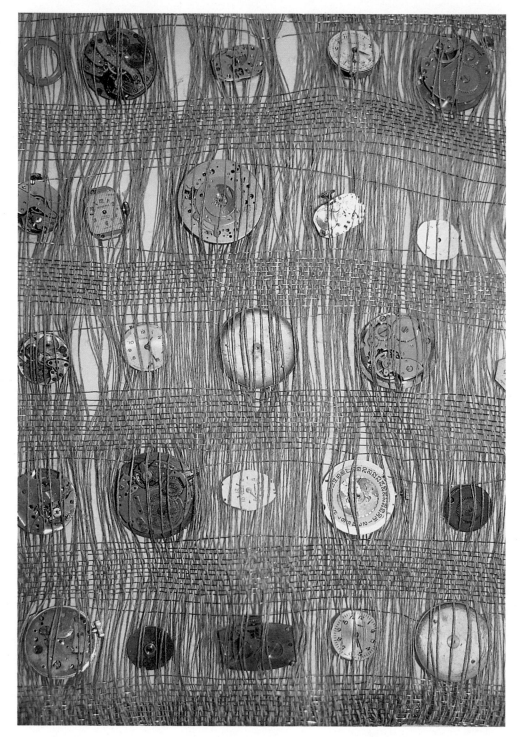

4. **Zoe Hope**	iron wire weft;
Caught in	watch parts
Time	Width
Handwoven	152.4cm (60in)
One-off	Height
Linen warp;	152.4cm (60in)

5. **Zoe Hope**
Daisy Chain
Hand leno-woven
and pressed fabric
Limited batch
production
Silk, daisies
Piece width
101.6cm (40cm)
Piece length
183cm (72in)

6. **Feliksas
   Jakubauskas**
   Juda's Coins
   Construction
   One-off
   Synthetic fibre,
   wire, plexiglass
   Width
   20cm (7⅞in)
   Height
   20cm (7⅞in)
   Depth
   20cm (7⅞in)

8. (Right) **Eta Sadar Breznik**
Fire (detail)
Handwoven
One-off
Rayon
Width
250cm (98⅜in)
Height
200cm (78⅜in)

9. (Far right)
Jan Truman
Suspended Structure
One-off
Knitted wire,
embroidery threads,
glass beads, found
objects
Width 30cm (11¾in)
Height 33cm (13in)
Depth 30cm (11¾in)

Textile artists absorbed in the creation of gauze-like three-dimensional structures play upon the tensions between sculptural volume and lack of weight; this contradictory lightness is further enhanced by light itself – flickering through, casting shadows, altering perceptions of density as the viewer moves. **Teresa Pla** uses ancient sprang and plaiting techniques to make hand-shaped 'Square Balls' that are rigid and yet fragile, and the fragility inherent in play-of-light sculptures also means that scale can be deceptive, as demonstrated by **Eta Sadar Breznik, Jan Truman** and **Feliksas Jakubauskas** – in works large, medium and small respectively.

7. **Teresa Pla**
Square Balls
Sprang, handshaped
construction
One-off
Cotton
Width 30cm (11¾in);
40cm (15⅜in) 50cm
(19⅝in)
Height 30cm (11¾in);
40cm (15⅜in); 50cm
(19⅝in)
Depth 30cm (11¾in);
40cm (15⅜in) 50cm
(19⅝in)

11. (Top left & right)
Iben Brøndum
Untitled
Handpainted resist,
double sided
One-off
Silk crêpe de Chine
Width repeat
0.9cm (⅓in)
Length repeat
4cm (1½in)

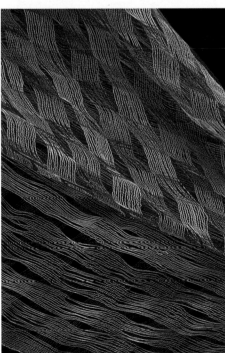

12. **Luis Omar Acosta**
Far left: *Waves of
Fire in the Earth*
Wool warp; silk weft
Left: *Transparent
Symphony*
Sewing machine-
stitched construction
One-off
Rayon
Piece width
140cm (55in)
Piece length
140cm (55in)

10. (Left) **Louise Sass**
Flow 2
Hand print with
mechanical resist
Prototype
Cotton
Piece width
146cm (57½in)
Piece length
250cm (98⅜in)
Width repeat
120cm (47⅛in)
Length repeat
53.5cm (21in)

14. Diann Parrott
Until I Die
Hand screen,
found objects and
monotype print
One-off
Cotton muslin
Width
114.3cm (45in)
Height
731cm (288in)

13. Ray Pierotti
Untitled
Handpainted
furnishing fabric
One-off
Colourfast Inkodye,
acrylic paint, oil-
based colour
pencil on cotton
Width
122cm (48in)
Height
366cm (144in)

15. (Right)
Jette Nevers
Facet
Machine-woven
bedding
Mercerized cotton
Standard bedding
sizes
Manufacturer:
Georg Jensen A/S,
Denmark

18. **Ulf Moritz**
Lunaris
Machine-woven
semi-sheer
50 per cent polyester,
39 per cent cotton,
6 per cent polyamide,
5 per cent Lurex
Piece width
155cm (61in)
Manufacturer: Sahco
Hesslein, Germany

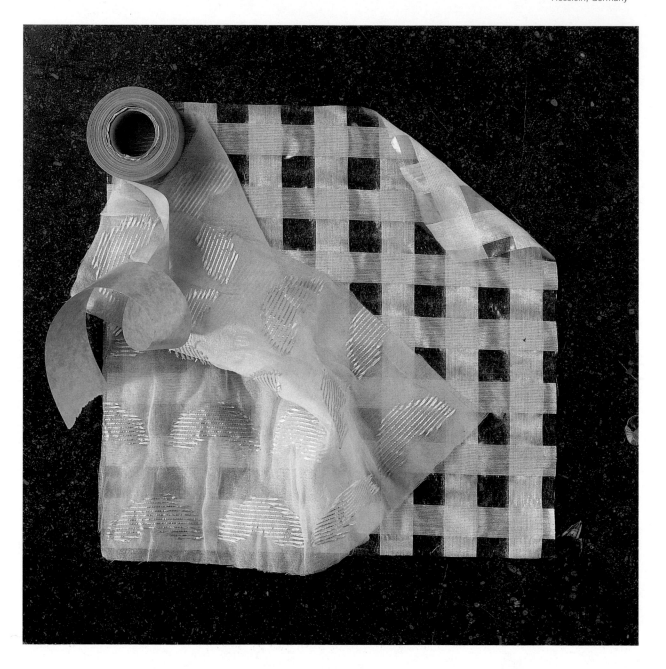

17. **Ulf Moritz**
Candidus
Machine-woven
semi-sheer
40 per cent polyester,
31 per cent cotton,
24 per cent viscose,
5 per cent polyamide
Piece width
155cm (61in)
Manufacturer: Sahco
Hesslein, Germany

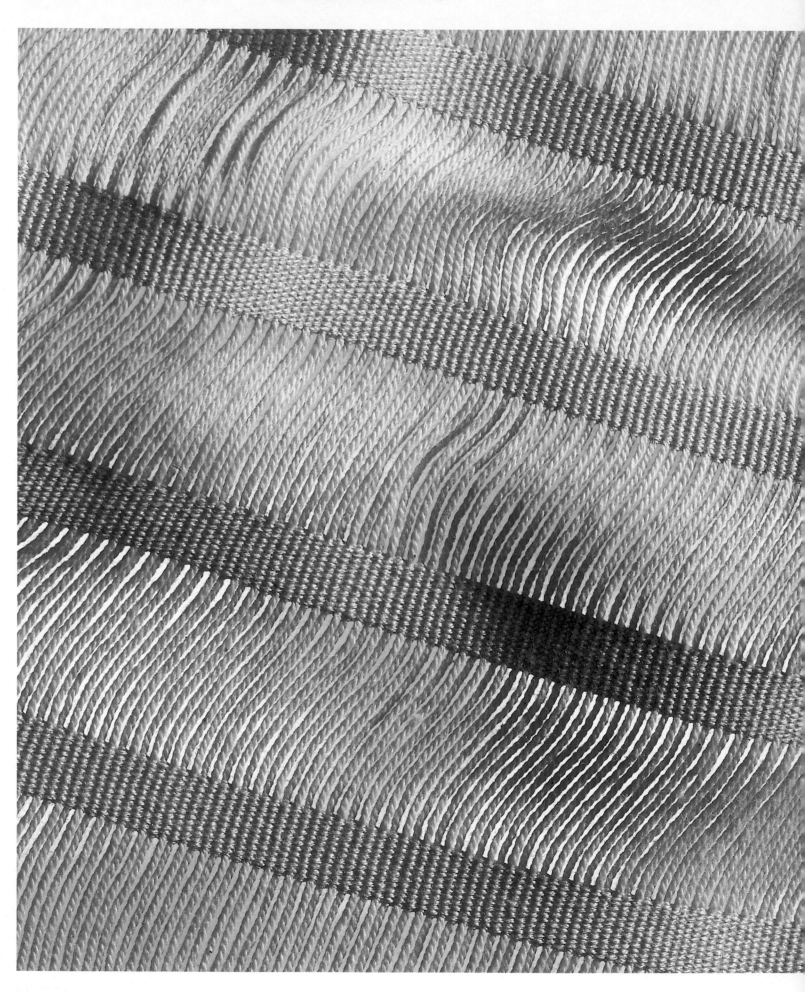

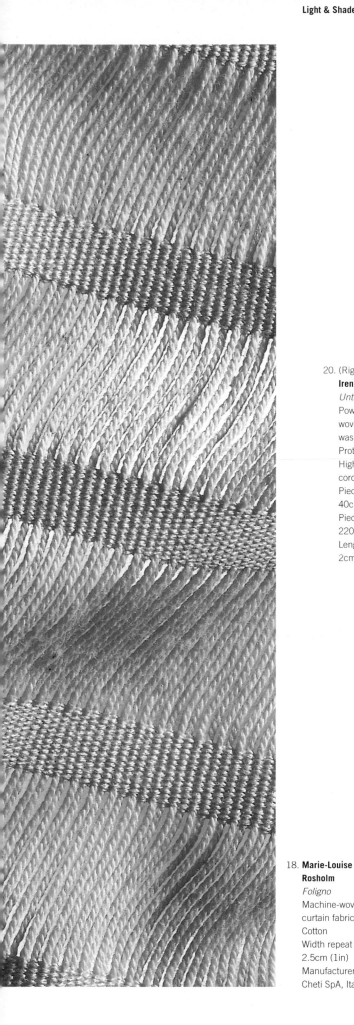

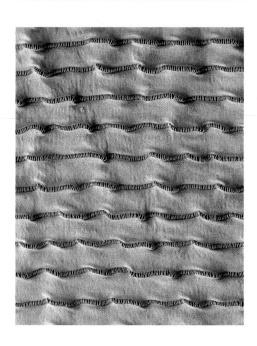

19 **Junichi Arai**
Untitled (detail)
Woven fabric
One-off
Polyester,
bonded polyester
film, bonded
aluminium film
Width
700cm (275½in)
Height
2,800cm (1,102in)
Weight 3.5kg (7¾lb)

20. (Right)
Irene Paskvalic
Untitled
Power-dobby
woven, shrink
washed
Prototype
High-twist cotton,
cord-dyed linen
Piece width
40cm (15¾in)
Piece length
220cm (86⅝in)
Length repeat
2cm (¾in)

21. **Irene Paskvalic**
Untitled
Power-dobby
woven, with cut
weft floats
Prototype
Wool ground warp
and weft, chenille
cotton yarn pattern
weft
Piece width
145cm (57⅛in)
Piece length
100cm (39⅜in)
Width repeat
6cm (2¼in)
Length repeat
6cm (2¼in)

18. **Marie-Louise
Rosholm**
Foligno
Machine-woven
curtain fabric
Cotton
Width repeat
2.5cm (1in)
Manufacturer: Fede
Cheti SpA, Italy

23. Sue Timney and Grahame Fowler
Magic Flute
Devoré velvet
Cotton
Piece width
112cm (44in)
Manufacturer:
Timney-Fowler
Ltd, UK

22. Maryke Arp
A half a circle
(detail)
Construction
One-off
Tyvek, transparent
synthetic,
various threads
Diameter
25cm (9¾in)

24. Finn Sködt
Torij
Reactive-printed
curtain fabric
Trevira CS
Width repeat
140cm (55in)
Length repeat
56cm (22in)
Manufacturer:
Kvadrat Boligtextiler
A/S, Denmark

25. (Right)
Robert Lamarre
Shalom
Hand screen-
printed burn-out
Limited batch
production
Pes, rayon,
pearlescent pigment
Width repeat
135cm (53⅛in)
Length repeat
80cm (31½in)

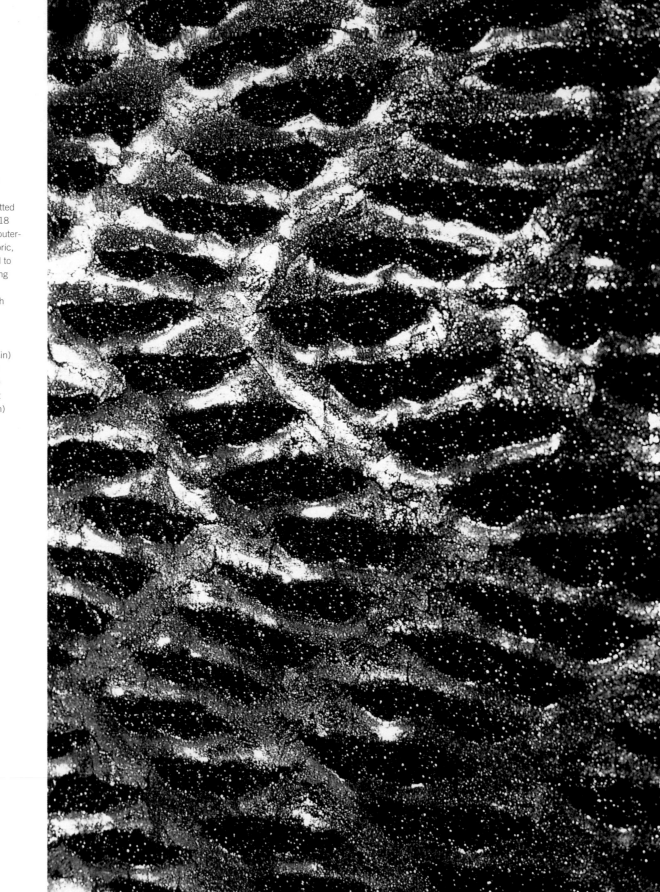

26. **Gary Rooney**
Coal
Machine-knitted
(Moratronic 18
gauge) computer-
designed fabric,
heat pressed to
almost melting
point
Limited batch
production
Lurex, wool
Piece width
110cm (43¼in)
Piece length
15cm (5⅞in)
Width repeat
30cm (11¾in)

27. **Gary Rooney**
Scales
Jersey machine-knitted (Moratronic 18 gauge) computer-designed fabric, heat calendered and pigment printed
Limited batch production
Lycra, Courtelle
Piece width 110cm (43¼in)
Width and length repeat 6cm (2¼in)

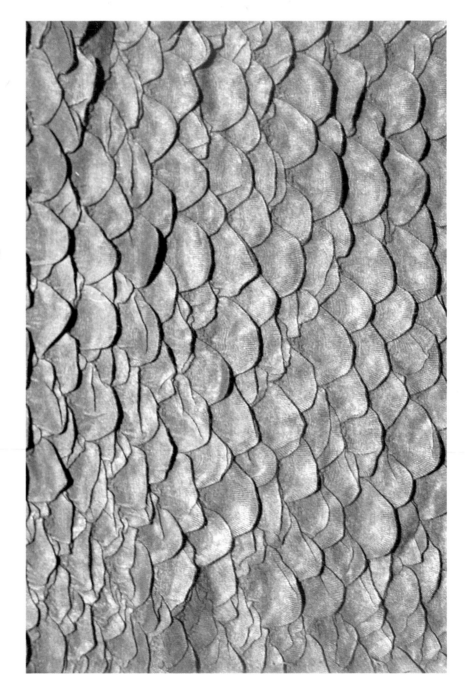

28. **Reiko Sudo**
Floe
Jacquard weave
49 per cent cotton,
51 per cent wool
Width 92cm
(36⅛in)
Width repeat
9cm (3½in)
Length repeat
17cm (6⅝in)
Manufacturer:
Nuno Corporation,
Japan

29. **Pat Hodson**
Blue Flame
Wax-resist,
dyed panel
(part of series)
One-off
Fibre-reactive
dye on cotton
Width
122cm (48in)
Height
114.3cm (45in)

30. (Right) **Isabella
Whitworth**
Mythic Themes
Resist-worked
scarves
One-off
Habotai, twill,
crêpe de Chine
silks, Kniazeff
dyes
Width
20.3cm (8in)
Height
137.2cm (54in)

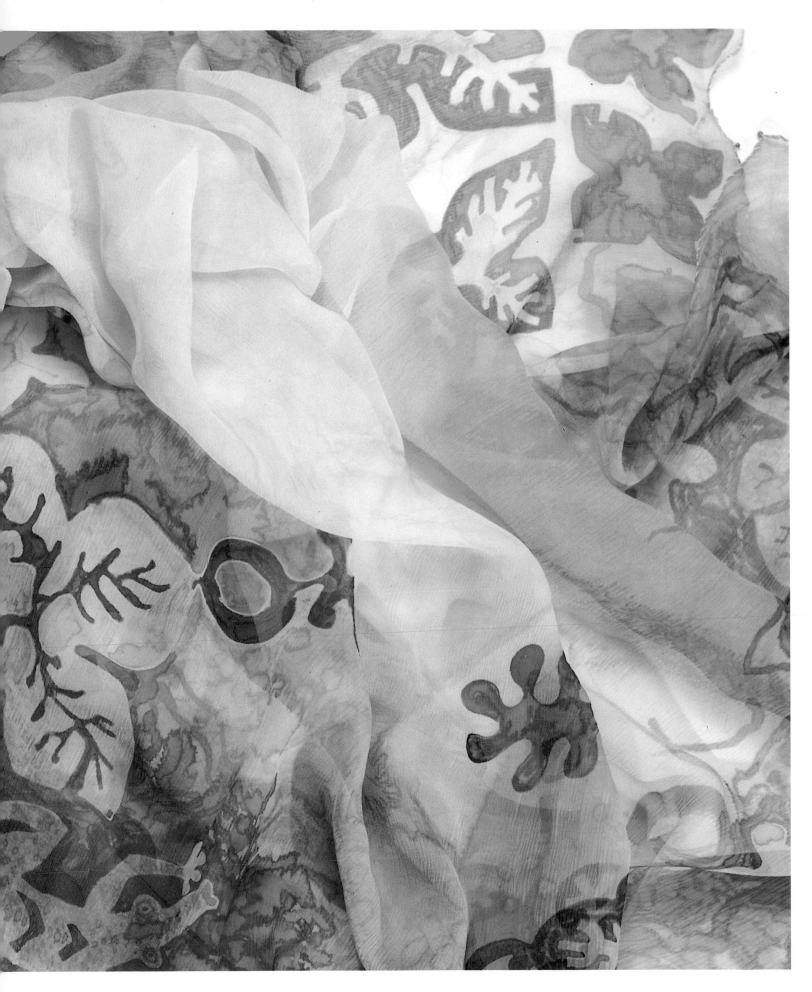

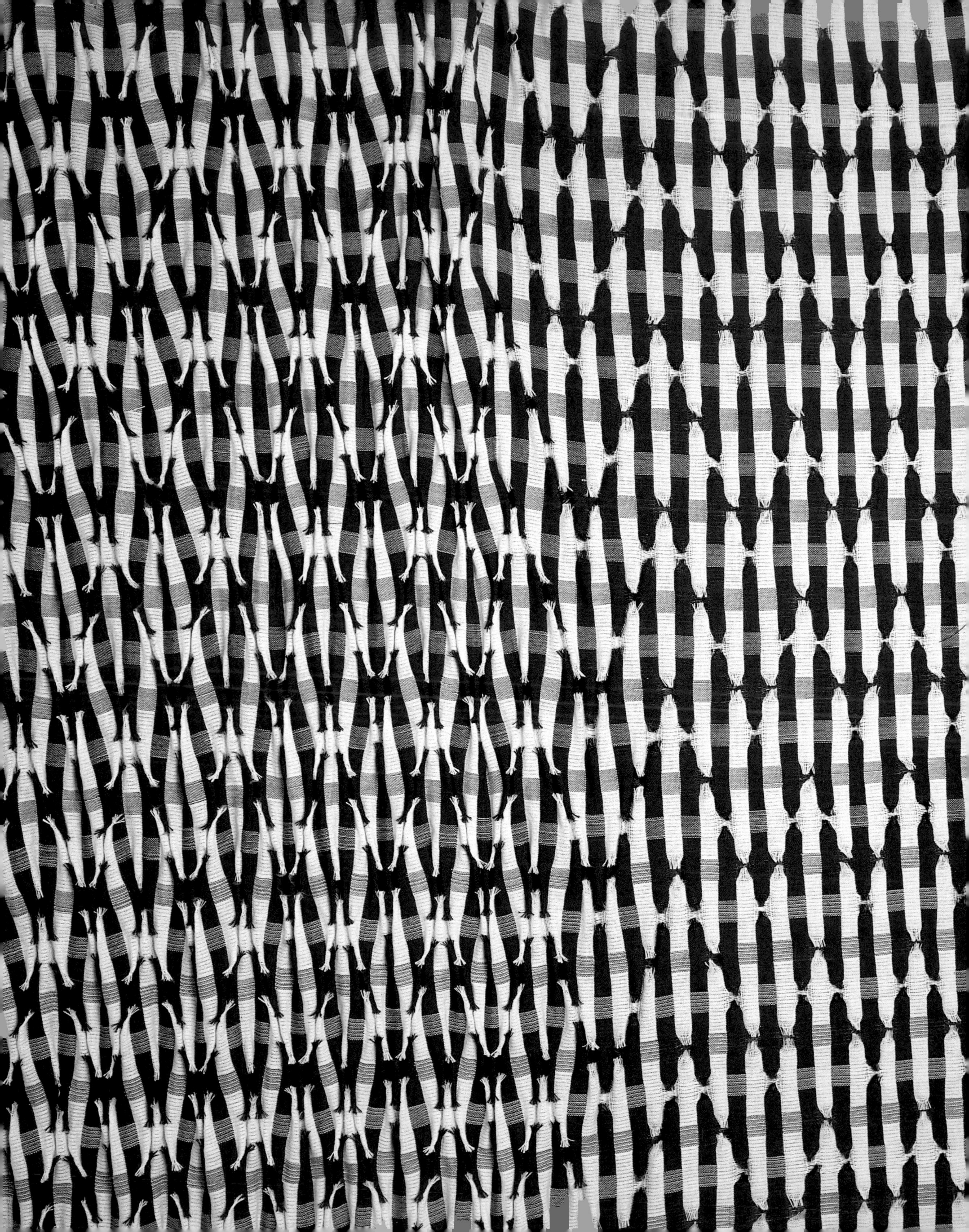

1. (Left) **Tina Moor**
Two States I
Handwoven
doublecloth
Prototype
Polyester 100/2 dtex
Piece width
80cm (31½in)
Piece length
150cm (59in)
Width repeat
8cm (3⅛in)
Length repeat
3cm (1in)

Section

③ ● **Earth**

2. (Above) **Penny Carey Wells**
Daily Tribune
Construction
One-off
Handmade paper, dyes, pigments, string
Width 50cm (19⅝in)
Height 70cm (27⅝in)
Depth 10cm (3⅞in)

The three-dimensional qualities of textiles provide innovative makers and designers with both challenge and opportunity. An undulating terrain comes naturally to textiles, and today the emphasis is on the enhancement of that property through a wide range of techniques that suggest, and often replicate, ploughed furrows, crazed or distressed earth, tyre tracks or volcanic surfaces. Such texture, rather than imagery, is the key feature of avant-garde fashion fabrics, but the use of this approach permeates all areas.

The inherent characteristics of fibres provide a wide range of effects. The juxtaposition of fibres with different shrinkage rates, or of the same fibre in overspun and 'normal' yarns, can create crushed, crinkled or furrowed fabrics once washed, and Drahomira Hampl's fabrics can be reformed by washing again and pressing. Unpredictably shrunken and buckled textures are produced by Junichi Arai, who ties as if about to tie-dye but omits the dyeing, tumble drying instead; he also creates subtle texture of a different sort by incorporating wool into lamé cloths that are tied to protect areas to remain metallic during 'melt-off' and dyeing.

Other methods used to entrap three-dimensional relief include the 'accidental' slippage exploited by Margot Rolf in her computer-Jacquard embroidered cloths. The incorporation of 'accidents' can also be appreciated in Joaquim Verdu's witty manipulation of machine knits for Canet

Punt; in contrast, relief knitting by Kazimiera Frymark-Blaszczyk creates subtle variety across a stretchy grid of mounds. Pile also readily accedes to sculpting, whether into the formal 'tracks' by Peter Maly for Jab, or the wild loops of Gloria Crouse's hooked rugs. Computer-controlled mechanisms are not only well integrated into innovative embroidery design, but also prove useful tools for print and weave designers. The latter include Cynthia Schira, who uses a Dornier computerized Jacquard loom to combine the qualities of drawn lines with hard-edged ribbed weave shapes, exploiting the resulting shadow for added visual interest. Helle Abild creates three-dimensional, layered illusions on computer, printing out and heat-transferring to cloth.

The ultimate exploration of sculptural form is represented by four artists from opposite sides of the world. In Australia, Penny Carey Wells manipulates handmade paper into 'books about books'. Grethe Wittrock's paper 'kimonos' typify the abstraction of body form that characterizes a strong strand of Danish interests; in Britain, Jane Harris uses pleating to create mysterious shroud-like body coverings, tie-dyeing to form tissue-like silks, which she also turns into kinetic structures exploring natural elements such as wind and light. Hiu Shi, in China, works with a wide range of materials in sculptures that interact with the earth in both literal and spiritual terms.

3. **Jane Harris**
Untitled
Tie-dyed
construction
(detail)
One-off
Habotai silk
Width
50cm (19⅝in)
Height
180cm (70⅞in)

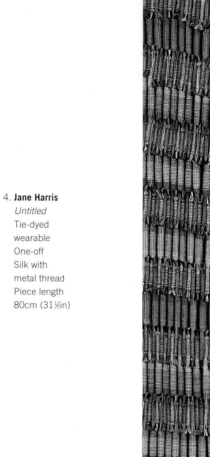

4. **Jane Harris**
Untitled
Tie-dyed
wearable
One-off
Silk with
metal thread
Piece length
80cm (31½in)

5. **Jane Harris**
Untitled
Tie-dyed
construction
(detail)
One-off
Habotai silk
Width
50cm (19⅝in)
Height
180cm (70⅞in)

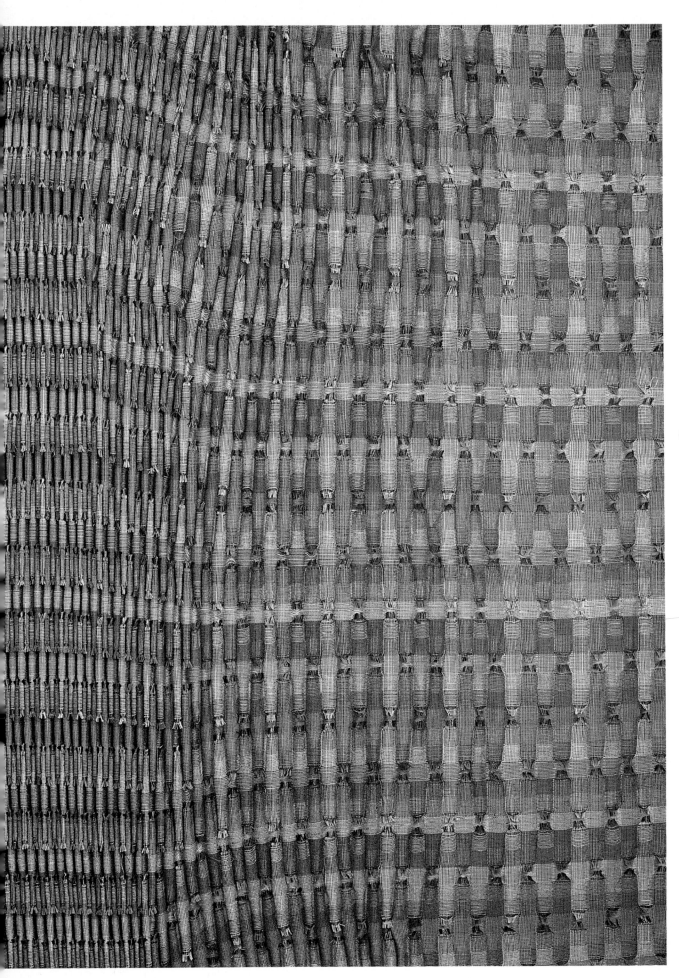

6. **Tina Moor**
   Two States II
   Handwoven
   doublecloth
   Prototype
   Polyester 100/2 dtex
   Piece width
   80cm (31⅓in)
   Piece length
   150cm (59in)
   Width repeat
   8cm (3⅛in)
   Length repeat
   3cm (1⅛in)

7. (Left) **Ann Richards**
Pleat Chequerboard
Handwoven, hand-
dyed doublecloth,
wet finished
Limited batch
production
Linen, silk
Piece width
28cm (11in)
Piece length
155cm (61in)

8. (Left and above)
Grethe Wittrock
Kamiko
Handwoven
specifically for
kimono/clothes
Prototype
Paper yarn made
from abaca
Made to measure
Designer of kimono/
clothes Ann Schmidt-
Christensen

11. **Drahomira Hampl**
Bubbles
Handwoven
curtain fabric
Limited batch
production
Cotton, polyester
Piece width
25cm (9¾in)
Piece length
27cm (10⅝in)

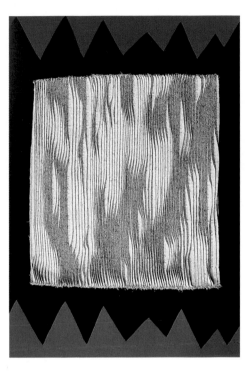

10. **Drahomira Hampl**
Ribs
Handwoven
folded fabric
Limited batch
production
Cotton
Piece width
47cm (18½in)
Piece length
52cm (20½in)

9. (Left) **Drahomira Hampl**
Interlacing
Doublewoven
furnishing fabric
Limited batch
production
Cotton, wool
Piece width
47cm (18½in)
Piece length
52cm (20½in)

Doublecloth offers an ideal method of creating intermingled areas of different texture and tension because it creates, as its name implies, two layers of cloth. By manipulating weave structure, shrinkage rates of different yarns, or points of intersection, a wide range of effects are created. **Eiji Miyamoto** (pages 64, 65) continues the Japanese-led exploration of doublecloth, but its potential has fuelled imaginations around the world; the extraordinary range of possibilities inform the work of many weavers, including **Drahomira Hampl**, **Ann Richards** (page 60) and **Irene Paskvalic** (page 67). Some clip areas to further enliven the surface; **Tina Moor** (page 59) partly cuts threads to allow the cloth to be distorted, until pulled in the other direction.

12. Reiko Sudo
Spanish Moss
Jacquard weave
35 per cent silk,
65 per cent wool
Piece width
35cm (13¾in)
Piece length
160cm (63in)
Manufacturer: Nuno
Corporation, Japan

15. (Right)
Eiji Miyamoto
Untitled
Machine-shrunk
woven fabric
One-off
Cotton, linen, silk
Piece width
80cm (31½in)
Manufacturer:
Miyashin Co.
Ltd, Japan

13. Eiji Miyamoto
Untitled
Machine-shrunk
doubleweave
One-off
Cotton, wool
Piece width
100cm (39⅜in)
Manufacturer:
Miyashin Co. Ltd,
Japan

14. (Right)
Ann Richards
Square Waves
Handwoven and
hand-dyed
doublecloth,
wet finished
Limited batch
production
Silk, wool
Piece width
33cm (13in)
Piece length
160cm (63in)

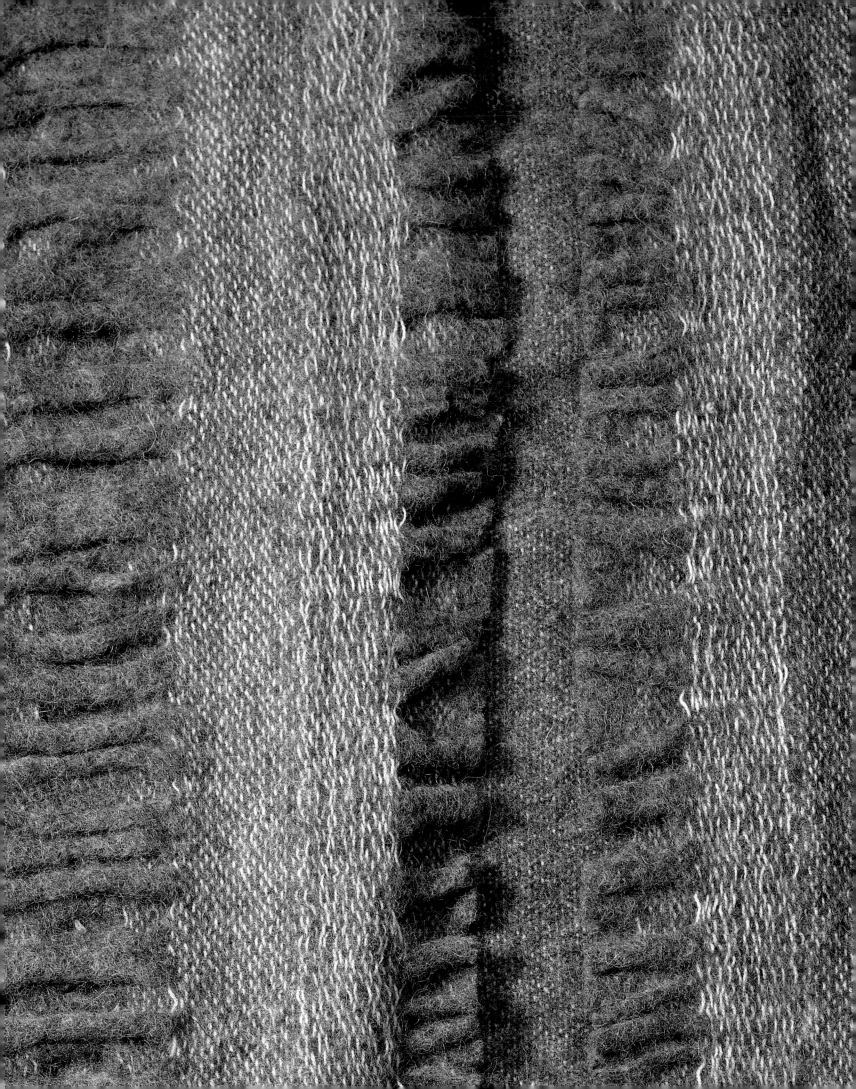

16. (Left) **Eiji Miyamoto**
Chemical
Contract-woven
fabric with
chemically induced
shrunken weft
One-off
Polyester cotton
warp; polyester weft
Piece width
100cm (39⅜in)
Manufacturer:
Miyashin Co.
Ltd, Japan

18. (Right)
Irene Paskvalic
Untitled
Hand dobby-woven
doublecloth
Prototype
Mercerized
cotton, cotton,
handspun silk
Piece width
120cm (47⅛in)
Piece length
230cm (90½in)
Width repeat
3cm (1⅛in)
Length repeat
3.5cm (1⅜in)

19. (Below)
Irene Paskvalic
Untitled
Hand-dobby woven
doublecloth
Prototype
Mercerized cotton,
cotton, chenille
Piece width
48cm (18⅞in)
Piece length
160cm (63in)
Width repeat
1.5cm (½in)
Length repeat
2.5cm (1in)

17. **Irene Paskvalic**
Untitled
Hand dobby-
woven doublecloth
Prototype
Mercerized cotton,
cotton, linen, wool
Piece width
45cm (17⅝in)
Piece length
230cm (90½in)
Width repeat
1.5cm (½in)
Length repeat
1cm (⅜in)

20. **Joaquim Verdu**
Machine plain
knit 100 per
cent acrylic
Manufacturer:
Canet Punt
S.A.L., Spain

21. (Right) **Almira Sadar
and Marija Jenko**
Snow Queen
Relief-moulded felt
textile/garment
Prototype
Polyester fibre
Piece width
80cm (31½in)
Piece length
180cm (70⅞in)

23. (Right) **Kazimiera
Frymark-Blaszczyk**
Land
Hand/machine knit
One-off
Polyamide
Width repeat
9cm (3½in)
Length repeat
11.5cm (4½in)
Manufacturer: High
School of Fine Arts
and Design in
Lodz, Poland

22. **Hella Jongerius**
Moulded bath mat
Limited batch
production
Polyurethane
Length 55.8cm
(21⅞in)
Width 39cm
(15⅓in)
Manufacturer:
Droog Design,
The Netherlands

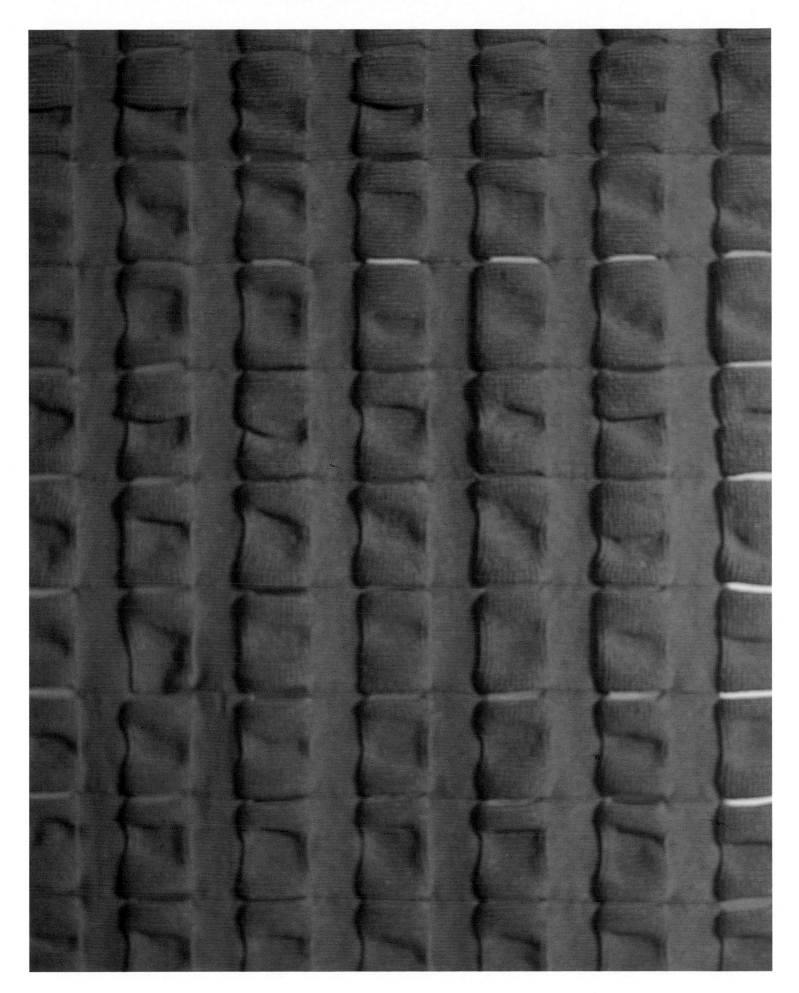

24. **Peter Maly**
Match
Machine-made
wall-to-wall carpet
Pure wool, brass/
refined steel,
leather, silk
Manufacturer:
Jab Anstoetz-
Teppiche,
Germany

25. **Penny Carey Wells**
Sacred Ground
Construction
One-off
Handmade paper,
dyes, gold leaf
Width 50cm (19⅝in)
Height 60cm (23⅝in)
Depth 5cm (2in)

27. **Hui Shi**
Nest
Construction
One-off
Pulp, cotton,
bamboo strips
.Width
300cm (118in)
Height
240cm (94½in)
Unit height
60cm (23⅝in);
50cm (19⅝in);
45cm (17⅝in)
Diameter
100cm (39⅜in);
85cm (33⅜in);
80cm (31½in)

28. **Gloria Crouse**
Razzle-Dazzle
Handhooked rug
Limited batch
production
Cotton, satin,
polyester, paint,
latex, cut yardage
and yarn on
linen ground
Width 170.2cm
(67In)
Height 170.2cm
(67in)
Depth 5cm (2in)

29. **Gloria Crouse**
Polly Esther
Handhooked rug
Limited batch
production
Polyester, translucent
fibre, acrylics, paint,
cut yardage and yarn
Width 165.1cm
(65in)
Height 165.1cm
(65in)
Depth 5cm (2in)

26. (Left) **Katrin Hielle**
Beau
Jacquard weave
Limited batch
production
92 per cent virgin
wool, 6 per cent
polyamide, 2 per
cent viscose
Piece width
130cm (51⅛in)
Width repeat
0.8cm (⅓in)
Length repeat
1.8cm (⅝in)
Manufacturer:
Rohi Stoffe GmbH
Germany

30. (Left & below)
Helle Abild
Strings; Velvet
Computer-
generated heat-
transferred prints
One-off
Cotton
Width repeat
5 – 7.6cm (2 – 3in)
Length repeat
5 – 7.6cm (2 – 3in)

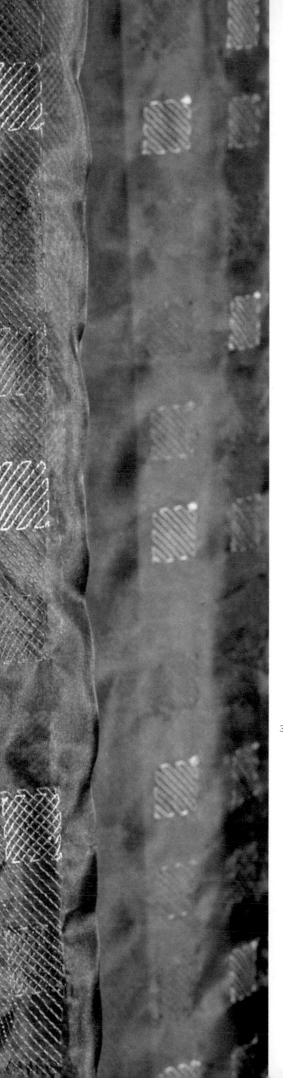

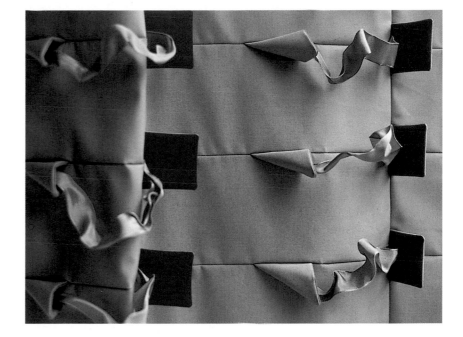

32. **Karol Pichler**
Green Lion Feeds Red Lion
Machine-sewn hanging
Prototype
Cotton, metallic ribbon
Piece width 60cm (23⅝in)
Piece length 70cm (27½in)
Width repeat 15cm (5⅞in)
Length repeat 30cm (11¾in)

31. **Margot Rolf**
Untitled
Computer-guided machine-embroidered three-layered curtain fabric
Prototype
Medeira/Aida organza, yarn
Piece width 140cm (55in)
Piece length 365cm (143⅜in)
Width repeat 52cm (20½in)
Length repeat 52cm (20½in)
Manufacturer: ZSK, Zangs Stickerei Krefeld, Germany

33. **Cynthia Schira**
Piceous
Computerized
Jacquard weave
Limited batch
production
Cotton
Piece width
140cm (55in)
Width repeat
70cm (27½in)
Length repeat
57cm (22⅜in)
Manufacturer:
Müller Zell GmbH
and Co., Germany

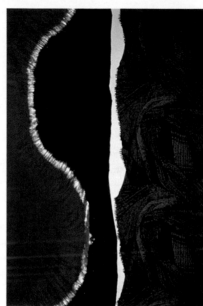

34. **Junichi Arai**
Untitled
Far left: Hand and
machine woven fabric
60 per cent wool,
40 per cent nylon
Left: Hand and
machine processed
fabric
One-off
Melted wool and
synthetic weft; nylon
film warp

35. **Meiny Vermaas-
van der Heide**
*Earth Quilt No. 27,
Fields of Colour IX*
Machine-pieced
and quilted
One-off
Cotton
Width
208.3cm (82in)
Height
121.9cm (48in)

36. (Right)
Silvia Heyden
*Simultaneous
Motion* (detail)
Tapestry
One-off
Linen, wool
Height 157cm
(61¾in)
Length 124cm
(48¾in)

1. (Left) **Yoshiki
Hishinuma**
Untitled (detail)
Hand-knitted wool,
cut into pieces and
hand-stitched to
slub yarn, pressed
One-off
Lamb's wool,
wool slub yarn
Made to measure
Manufacturer:
Hishinuma Associates
Co. Ltd, Japan

Section

④ # Raw Materials

2. **Reiko Sudo**
Shifu
Jacquard weave
52 per cent silk,
20 per cent cotton,
23 per cent paper
(Washi), 5 per cent
polyurethane
Piece width
70cm (27½in)
Manufacturer: Nuno
Corporation, Japan

A change of fibre or the method of turning it into yarn can alter otherwise identical cloths. Wiry or fuzzy, soft or springy, the final visual and tactile sensation is also dependent on the interaction of fibre, construction and finishing technique. These choices confront everyone who creates textiles, but are more evident in the seemingly simple cloths that rely on the character of fibres and yarns.

By exploiting the brightness of rayon against matt polyester, Hiroshi Awatsuji creates delicate textures. Using wool's tendency to felt, Yoshiki Hishinuma produces muzzy, indistinct forms; wool is also selected by Bodil Kellermann to survive the violent milling and napping that transforms coarse weaves into Kvadrat blankets saturated with colour. 'Pile' of various kinds – Carrara's terry bathrobes, Jackytex's open knits, or the chenille in, among others, Suzin Steerman's cloths for Knoll – adds richness of both tone and texture, and Ingrid Enarsson's bristling towers rely on the character of sisal, the colours applied by her unique spray-gun technique. Feliksas Jakubauskas, in 'Memorial to Indira Gandhi', releases polyester fibre to express form.

Many textiles in this group are handwoven. Chiaki and Kaori Maki, who together make up the Maki Textile Studio in Japan, have made a conscious decision to have their fabrics handwoven because they see that with merchants in pursuit only of low-cost production, 'high and fine craftsmanship is disappearing in this part of the planet. Our principle is to create new textiles that fit the modern Japanese and Western life using the best of Asian materials and hand work.' Central to their philosophy is the handspun wild (or tussah) silk incorporated into textural cloths made by Indian weavers who work exclusively for them; the natural irregularity of this yarn is given room to gurgle through the cloth like endless sparkling streams.

Silk, or silk combined with cashmere, is also used by the Norwegian weaver Jorun Schumann, but here it is thrown silk, providing both strength and sheen in soft, light fabrics constructed to enhance their draping qualities. In contrast, fibres appreciated for their brusque qualities include Icelandic two-ply washed and brushed woollen yarn used by Gudrún Gunnarsdóttir to make unusually wiry rugs; hand dyed horsehair worked into rugs by Colombian weavers using the Gobelin tapestry technique to interpret Kristin Carlsen Rowley's designs; and sisal and flax, which Karin Carlander manipulates using one of the oldest known but little-used rug-weaving techniques, taquette.

4. **Yoshiki Hishinuma**
Untitled
Pressed computer-
controlled
embroidery
One-off
Wool slub yarn
Manufacturer:
Hishinuma
Associates Co.
Ltd, Japan

3. **Jackytex Tessuti
a Maglia**
*Gregor 806, Nepal
82*
Gregor 806:
Machine-knitted
fashion fabric
54 per cent wool,
46 per cent nylon
Piece width
110cm (43¼in)

Nepal 82:
Machine-jersey
knitted fashion fabric
58 per cent viscose,
18 per cent polyester,
24 per cent nylon
Piece width
105cm (41½in)
Manufacturer: Jackytex
Tessuti a Maglia, Italy

5. (Right) **Yoshiki
Hishinuma**
Untitled
Hand-pressed
and trodden
shrunken wool
One-off
Wool
Made to measure
Manufacturer:
Hishinuma
Associates Co.
Ltd, Japan

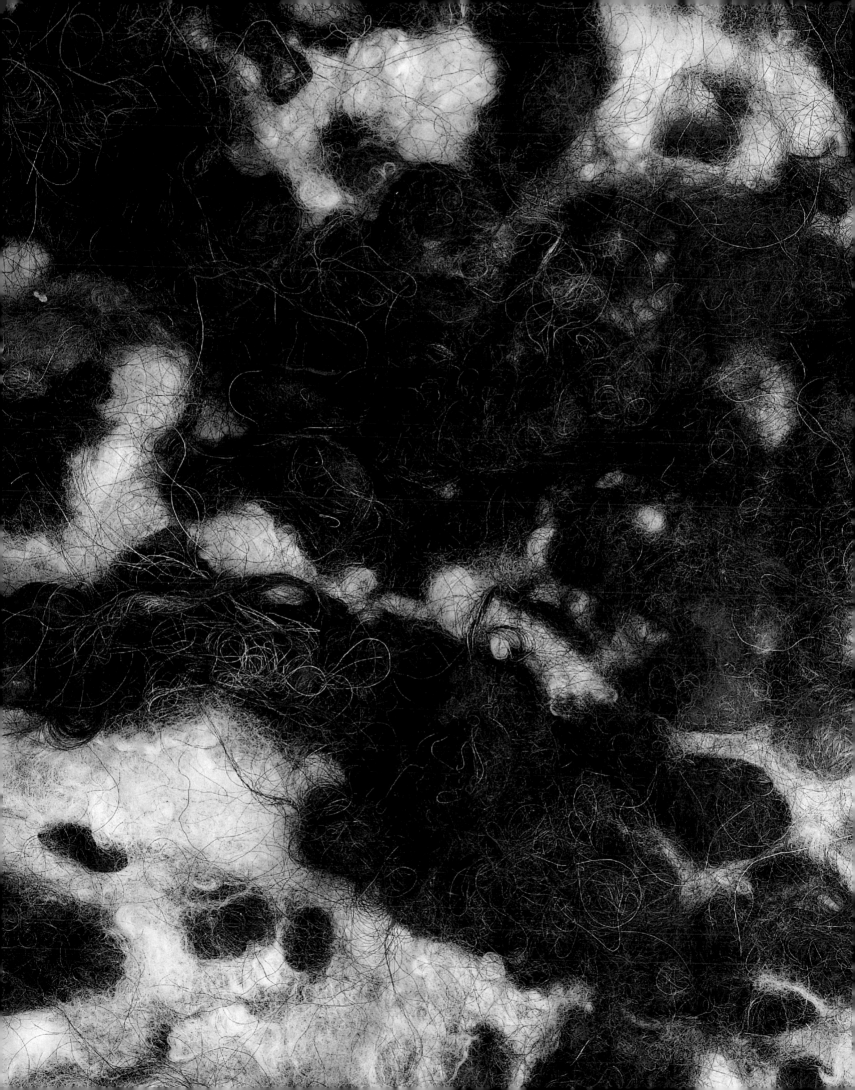

7. **Irene Paskvalic**
Untitled
Power dobby-
loom weave
Prototype
Unbleached
mercerized cotton
warp; unbleached
cotton, natural grey
and black wool weft
Piece width
120cm (47⅛in)
Piece length
70cm (27½in)
Width repeat
1.50cm (½in)
Length repeat
1cm (⅜in)

8. **Irene Paskvalic**
Untitled
Power dobby-
loom weave
Prototype
Unbleached cotton,
wool warp; unbleached
mercerized cotton weft
Piece width
80cm (31½in)
Piece length
160cm (63in)
Width repeat
2cm (¾in)
Length repeat
2cm (¾in)

6. (Left)
Hiroshi Awatsuji
Untitled
Yarn-dyed
Jacquard-woven
furnishing fabric
80 per cent polyester,
20 per cent rayon

Piece width
137cm (54in)
Piece length
500cm (196¾in)
Manufacturer:
Fujie Textile Co.
Ltd, Japan

10. **Simone Tremp**
Monika
Handpainted warp,
space-reeded
handwoven scarf
Prototype
Silk, dyes

Width repeat
3cm (1⅛in)
Length repeat
8cm (3⅛in)
Manufacturer: Simone
Tremp Textilatelier,
Switzerland

9. **Div. Indaco**
*Pasolini, Altman
Unito*
Machine-woven
fashion fabrics
Pasolini:
100 per cent
polyester
Piece width

145cm (57in)
Altman Unito:
70 per cent polyester
30 per cent nylon
Piece width
176cm (69¼in)
Manufacturer:
Achille Pinto SpA,
Div. Indaco, Italy

11. (Right) **Feliksas
Jakubauskas**
*Pro Memoriam
Indira Gandhi*
Construction
One-off
Synthetic fibre,
plexiglass
Height 20cm (7⅞in)
Width 20cm (7⅞in)
Depth 20cm (7⅞in)

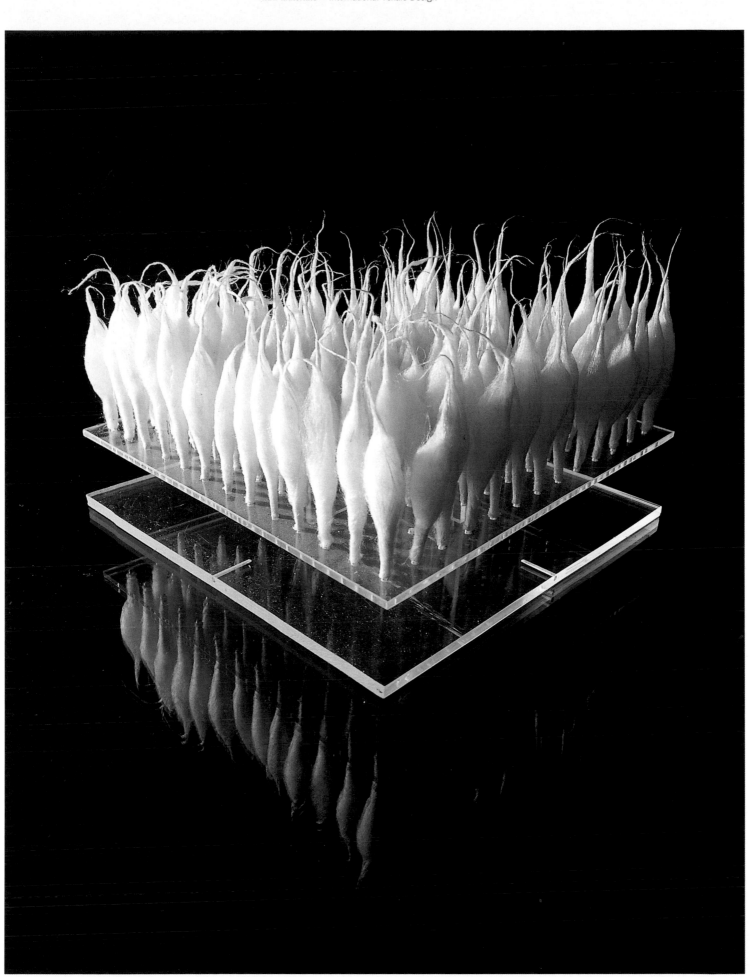

13. **Christie Dunning**
Rosepath Tie-up
Handwoven fabric
Wool weft; silk,
wool, mohair warp
Piece width
45.7cm (18in)
Piece length
137cm (54in)

14. **Jack Larsen**
Fielding
Doublewarped
Jacquard weave
Polyester
Piece width
112cm (44in)
Width repeat
6.4cm (2½in)
Length repeat
6.4cm (2½in)
Manufacturer: Jack
Lenor Larsen, USA

12. (Left)
Michelle Wild
Untitled
Handwoven and
finished samples
Prototype
Silk, wool, chenille
Width
17cm (6⅝in)
Length
17cm (6⅝in)

16. **Chiaki** and
Kaori Maki
Malda Akiha
Handweave
Limited batch
production
Natural colour
Malda silk,
natural-dyed wool
Piece width
80cm (31½in)
Piece length
200cm (78⅝in)
Manufacturer:
Maki Textile
Studio, Japan

15. **Chiaki Maki**
Little stream
Four-harness
handweave
One-off
Silk, handspun
wild silk, natural
indigo dye
Piece width
40cm (15¾in)
Piece length
150cm (59in)
Manufacturer:
Maki Textile
Studio, Japan

18. **Chiaki Maki**
Une
Hand-Jacquard weave
Limited batch
production
Wool, handspun
wild silk
Piece width
60cm (23⅝in)
Piece length
200cm (78¾in)
Width repeat
4cm (1½in)
Length repeat
12cm (4⅝in)
Manufacturer: Maki
Textile Studio, Japan

17. (Left) **Chiaki Maki**
Floats I
Hand-Jacquard
weave
Limited batch
production
Natural colour
wool, linen, hand-
spun wild silk
Piece width
60cm (23⅝in)
Piece length
200cm (78¾in)
Width repeat
5.6cm (2⅛in)
Length repeat
8cm (3⅛in)
Manufacturer: Maki
Textile Studio, Japan

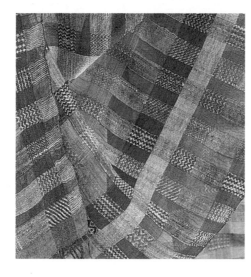

19. (Left & above)
Chiaki Maki
Shady
Hand-Jacquard weave
Natural-dyed wool,
linen, handspun
wild silk
Piece width
70cm (27½in)
Piece length
200cm (78¾in)
Width repeat
15cm (5⅞in)
Length repeat
45cm (17⅝in)
Manufacturer: Maki
Textile Studio, Japan

20. **Eva Fleg
Lambert**
Detail of hand-
spun, hand-dyed
Shilasdair yarns.

21. **Di Gilpin**
Kullu
Knitted jacket
(detail)
One-off
Shilasdair natural
grey and indigo-
dyed wool by
Eva Fleg Lambert
Made to measure

22. **Ingrid Enarsson**
Triologi
Construction
One-off
Steel and wire
net, sisal sprayed
with weather-
resistant paint
Heights
400cm (157⅜in)
450cm (177⅛in)
500cm (196⅞in)
Diameters
70cm (27½in)

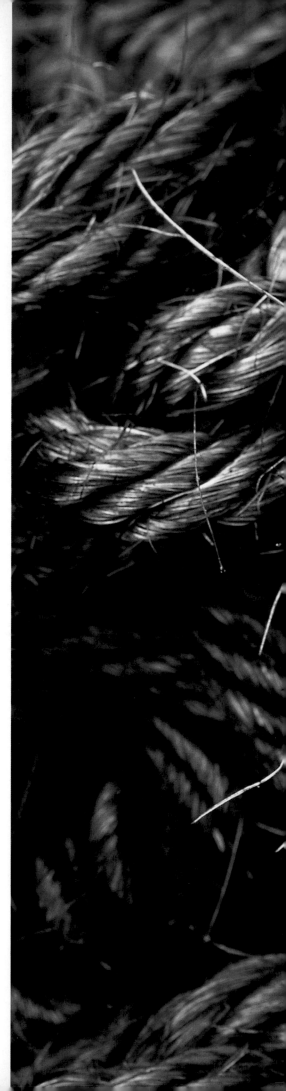

23. **Ingrid Enarsson**
Detail of hand-
dyed sisal.

25. **Anne Field**
Untitled
Handwoven
fleece rug
One-off
Natural-coloured
English Leicester
fleece, linen warp
Width
152.4cm (60in)
Height
101.6cm (40in)

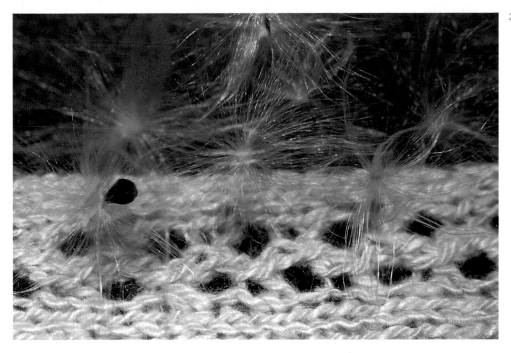

26. **Dora Yarid Murcia**
Untitled (detail)
Knitted sample
Natural-coloured
handspun fibre
obtained from
the fruit of the
Calotropis Procera

24. (Left) **Karin
Carlander**
Taquette
Taquette hand-
woven doormat
Prototype
Sisal, flax
Width
80cm (31½in)
Height
50cm (19⅝in)

The use of fibres unique to certain areas has been spurred on by ecological concerns. **Dora Yarid Murcia** reflects this by gathering, spinning and knitting with a natural fibre obtained from the fruit of the Calotropis Procera, a shrub that grows as a weed on the dry and poor lands of Colombia and provides a potentially significant source. This fibre is characterized by being softer, warmer, lighter and shinier than cotton; the resulting uneven thread is used in its natural state or with a weak colouring.

28. (Right)
Bodil Kellermann
Autuno
Machine-woven
rug
Wool
Width
140cm (55in)
Height
220cm (86⅝in)
Manufacturer:
Kvadrat Boligtextiler
A/S, Denmark

27. **Juha Laurikainen**
Potpuri
Handwoven blankets
Limited batch
production
Wool
Width
90cm (35⅜in)
Height
160cm (63in)
Manufacturer:
Wetterhoff Ltd,
Finland

34. (Left) **Gudrún Gunnarsdóttir**
Untitled
Machine-woven rug
Two-ply woollen
thread
Width
130cm (51⅛in)
Height
200cm (78⅜in)
Manufacturer:
Folda Ltd, Iceland

36. **Adriane Nicolaisen**
Windows
Computerized
dobby-loom weave
Limited batch
production
Rayon warp; rayon/
chenille, rayon/
silk weft
Piece width
121.9cm (48in)
Piece length
45.7m (150ft)
Width repeat
30.5cm (12in)
Length repeat
20.3cm (8in)
Manufacturer:
Handwoven
Webworks, USA

35. **Ulf Moritz**
Lavinia
Handtufted
carpet
Wool, silk, Lurex,
copper
Width
200cm (78⅜in)
Height
200cm (78⅜in)
Manufacturer: Oliver
Treutlein, Germany

38. Jorun Schumann
Fashion fabric
Handwoven on
computer counter-
march loom
Limited batch
production
Silk warp; 50 per
cent camel hair/50
per cent silk weft
Piece width
90cm (35⅜in)
Piece length
1500cm (590½in)

37. Jorun Schumann
Big Shawl
Handwoven on
computer counter-
march loom
Limited batch
production
Silk warp; 65 per
cent cashmere/35
per cent silk weft
Width
80cm (31½in)
Height
240cm (94½in)

41. (Right) **Sandra von Sneiden**
Making Tracks
Handwoven
One off
Mercerized
cotton, viscose
slub
Width
86cm (33⅞in)
Height
250cm (98⅜in)

39. **Anne Fabricius Møller**
Sterling
Doublesided
direct-reactive
resist print
Prototype
Flax
Piece width
140cm (55in)
Piece length
400cm (157⅜in)

40. **Anne Fabricius Møller**
Medium Check
Doublesided
direct-reactive
resist print
Prototype
Flax
Piece width
140cm (55in)
Piece length
400cm (157⅜in)

Section
5

The Antique World

2. **Phillip Stanton**
Estena Estudio
Printed fabric
100 per cent
Percale cotton
Piece width
240cm (94½in)
Manufacturer:
Marieta Textil,
Spain

1. (Left) **Romeo Gigli**
Theodora
Jacquard weave
52 per cent silk,
48 per cent linen
Piece width
137.2cm (54in)
Width repeat
22.9cm (9in)
Length repeat
20.3cm (8in)
Manufacturer:
Donghia Textiles
Co. Inc., USA

The document floral is dead. At least, this is the message coming from innovative designers and manufacturers around the world: it still holds pride of place in settings that demand a sensitive interpretation, but its influence on mainstream design has passed. Instead, history is regarded as a livelier landscape, full of incident, all of it man-made. So when 'something borrowed' makes its way into cloth it is manipulated in an unmistakably modern fashion.

In keeping with this renaissance in attitude, paintings provide a starting point for many, unafraid to liken the textile surface to canvases of the past. In Marieta's well-established series of modern fabrics and rugs, the witty 'still life' images by Phillip Stanton and Regina Saura are a case in point. In contrast, Timney-Fowler, well known for their interpretations of engraved images, have turned to Italian cinquecento paintings.

Italy, not surprisingly, features strongly as both a source of inspiration and the site of manufacture. Domes and ceilings become pattern on Jessica Trotman's silks, while Romeo Gigli's chosen starting place, the mosaics of Ravenna, highlights the growing interest in 'Byzantine' styles. Rubelli takes inspiration from Burano lace, and equally evident in sumptuous fabrics by Dedar is the influence of the great heritage of Italian velvets. Hidden in Marcato's own timeless velvets of today is the modernity of their Imperfix finish, making them crush proof, stain resistant and water repellent.

Surfaces gleam as if polished by age. Carolyn Quartermaine, master of the Enlightenment script, still devises new ways to jar sensibilities with her combination of pigments, silk and wood; pigment-golds and -silvers also give an elegant patina in mass-produced fabrics, such as Osborne & Little's simple stars, and add enlivening touches in batiks by Maria Osadchaya and Anna Tchernetskaya. Both metallic washes and stencils on metallic tissue grounds contribute to Elisabeth Mann's richly distressed surfaces.

The fresh approach to history has also turned attention to pattern-making techniques of the past. The design team of Missakian/Contarsy are known for just such collections, created for mills around the world; shown here are their Jacquard and dobby weaves for the Fujie Textile Company, in which the elegance of an embossed moire finish is superimposed on yarn-dyed 'basic' stripes. Glenn Peckman – inspired by Guatemalan textiles – merges the complexity of handweaves with modern technology, and in similar vein Bozena Burgielska derives bold pattern and colour from Polish rug-making traditions.

3. **Sue Timney,**
   Grahame Fowler
   Studies
   Rotary screen print
   Cotton
   Width repeat
   133cm (52⅜in)
   Length repeat
   73.6cm (28⅞in)
   Manufacturer:
   Timney-Fowler
   Ltd, UK

4. (Right) **Sue Timney,**
   Grahame Fowler
   Librarian
   Rotary screen print
   Cotton
   Width repeat
   133cm (52⅜in)
   Length repeat
   102.2cm (40⅛in)
   Manufacturer:
   Timney-Fowler
   Ltd, UK

6. **Osborne & Little**
Alchemy Range
Machine screen-printed
Cotton, dyes, pigment
Piece widths
140cm (55in)
Length repeats
13 – 73cm
(5⅛in – 28⅝in)
Manufacturer:
Osborne & Little, UK

5. (Left) **Carolyn Quartermaine**
French Script
Hand print
Limited batch production
Silk taffeta, gold pigment
Piece width 122cm (48in)
Length repeat
100cm (39⅜in)
Manufacturer: Carolyn
Quartermaine, UK

7. **Patrizia Marcato**
Guardi
Imperfix-treated velvets
Permanent crush-
proof, stain-resistant
and water-repellent cotton
Piece width 140cm (55in)
Manufacturer: Luciano
Marcato srl, Italy

9. Dedar's Studio
Montefalco
Machine-woven
damask
66 per cent cotton,
34 per cent polyester
Piece width
140cm (55in)
Width repeat
35cm (13¾in)
Length repeat
31cm (12⅛in)
Manufacturer:
Dedar Srl, Italy

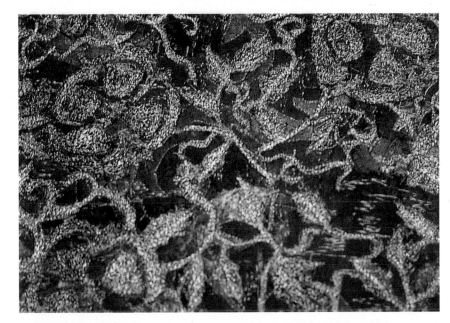

10. Elisabeth Mann
Antique Flora (detail)
Procion-dyed, patched
and piece-printed,
stencilled machine-
stitched cushions
Limited batch
production
Silk, cotton velvet,
metallic tissue,
procion dye
Width 40.6cm (16in)
Height 40.6cm (16in)

11. Elisabeth Mann
*Madrigal for
Sulgrave*
Hand-stitched,
printed, painted
and stencilled
Procion-dyed throw
One-off
Cotton, velvet, silk,
metallic tissue,
halizarin paint
Width
203cm (80in)
Height
140cm (55in)

8. (Left) **Elise Contarsy,
Anais Missakian**
*Colour Harmony
Collection*
Jacquard-woven, yarn-
dyed doublecloth, fialle
with embossed moire
finish
Polyester, cotton
Piece width
140 cm (55in)
Piece length
500cm (196¾in)
Manufacturer: Fujie
Textile Co. Ltd, Japan

12. **Lorenzo Rubelli SpA**
Modena
Machine weave
Skein-dyed viscose
Piece width
140cm (55in)
Manufacturer:
Lorenzo Rubelli
SpA, Italy

13. (Right)
Carol Westfall
Asobi
Jacquard weave
Limited batch
production
Polyester
Piece width
127cm (50in)
Width repeat
10.8cm (4¼in)
Length repeat
9.8cm (3⅞in)
Manufacturer:
Raxon Corporation,
USA

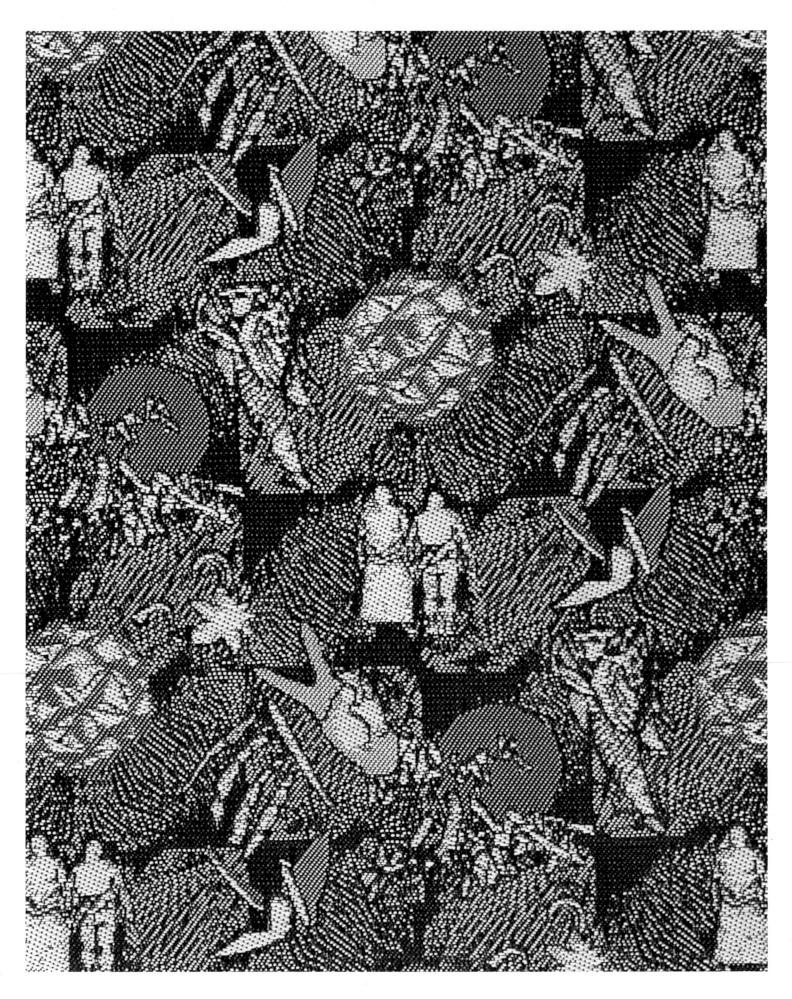

14. (Left) **Maria Osadchaya,
Anna Tchernetskaya**
Forgotten Romance
Batik panel
One-off
Cotton, aniline
dyes, paraffin
Width
240cm (94½in)
Height
330cm (129⅞in)

15. **Maria Osadchaya,
Anna Tchernetskaya**
Keeper
Batik panel
One-off
Cotton, aniline
dyes, paraffin
Width
240cm (94½in)
Height
360cm (141¾in)

16. **Jessica Trotman**
Untitled
Hand-discharged
and painted print
One-off
Raw silk,
printing dyes
Width
96.5cm (38in)
Height
91.4cm (36in)

17. **Ramm, Son
and Crocker**
*Festival/
Maypole*
Rotary screen
prints
Cotton
Festival:
Piece width
140cm (55in)

Length repeat
64cm (25⅛in)
Maypole:
Piece width
140cm (55in)
Length repeat
41cm (16⅛in)
Manufacturer:
Ramm, Son and
Crocker, UK

18. **Jessica Trotman**
Untitled
Hand screen-
printed fabric
One-off
Silk, velvet
Width
96.5cm (38in)
Height
91.4cm (36in)

19. **Bozena Burgielska**
Rainbow
Gripper Axminster
carpet
80 per cent wool,
20 per cent
polyamide
Piece width

200cm (78⅜in)
Piece length
200cm (78⅜in)
Repeats in multiples
of above sizes
Manufacturer:
Carpet
Factory, Poland

21. (Right) **Glenn
Peckman**
Jubilee
Machine
weave
Cotton
Piece width
137cm (54in)
Width repeat
56cm (22in)
Length repeat
18cm (7in)
Manufacturer:
Rodolph Inc,
USA

20. **Nina Laptchik**
Untitled
Art Protis collage
One-off
Wool, cotton
Width
158cm (62⅛in)
Height
182cm (71⅝in)

22. **Regina Saura**
Aroma
Machine-
tufted carpet
Wool
Width
240cm (94½in)
Height
170cm (66⅞in)
Manufacturer:
Marieta Textil,
Spain

23. Lynn Setterington
Distractions
Kantha/quilted panel
One-off
Dyed cotton cambric,
cotton perie threads
Width
83cm (32⅝in)
Height
65cm (25½in)

24. Natalka Shimin
Miss Inna
Tapestry
One-off
Wool, silver
thread
Width
80cm (31½in)
Height
150cm (59in)

25. **Fujie Textile
Design Studio**
Guilder, Rupiah, Mark
Warp-printed and
yarn-dyed dobby-
woven furnishing
fabrics
Polyester, cotton,
acrylic
Piece width
140cm (55in)
Manufacturer:
Fujie Textile Co.
Ltd, Japan

26. **G. P. & J. Baker**
Burma
Machine-woven
upholstery fabric
51 per cent cotton,
49 per cent viscose
Piece width
140cm (55in)
Repeat length
20cm (7⅞in)
Manufacturer:
G. P. & J. Baker, UK

27. **Pausa AG**
Venezuela,
Geometrie,
El Salvador
Machine screen
prints, linen
Width repeat
138cm (54½in)/
69cm (27⅛in)/

69cm (27⅛in)
Length repeat
91.4cm (36in)/
82cm (32¼in)/
82cm (32¼in)
Manufacturer:
Pausa AG,
Germany

The term 'document'
normally suggests
a floral pattern, but
examples from two
German companies
challenge this notion.
Reproducing wall-to-
wall carpets designed
by five Bauhaus
women, **Vorwerk**
was able not only to
provide patterns
intended as 'a pre-
cious fragment, a
living memory' of the
models for industry
produced at the
Bauhaus, but also to
work with three of the
designers themselves:
**Gertrud Arndt, Kitty
Fischer** (pages 134–5)
and **Monica Bella-
Broner**. And **Pausa**,
one of the firms which
originally produced
Bauhaus prototypes,
continue their 'anti-
floral' tradition with
a fresh look at Latin
American motifs.

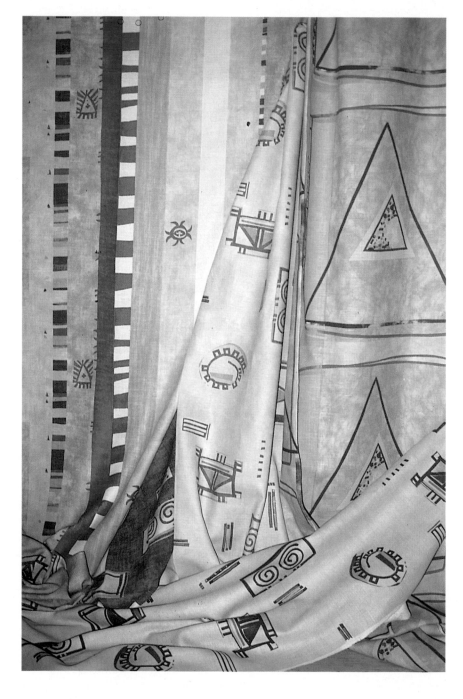

28. (Right) **Monica
Bella-Broner**
*Bauhaus Women –
from the Classic
range*
Machine-tufted
and printed heavy
contract carpet
Dupont's Antron
Classic polyamide
fibre
Width repeat
100cm (39⅜in)
Length repeat
95cm (37⅜in)
Manufacturer:
Vorwerk & Co.
Teppichwerke,
Germany

29. **Kitty Fischer**
Bauhaus Women –
from the Classic range
Machine-tufted
and printed heavy
contract carpet
Dupont's Antron
Classic polyamide
fibre
Width repeat
57cm (22⅜in)
Length repeat
32cm (12½in)
Manufacturer:
Vorwerk & Co.
Teppichwerke,
Germany

30. (Far right)
Gertrud Arndt (design)
Bauhaus Women –
from the Classic range
Machine-tufted
and printed heavy
contract carpet
Dupont's Antron
Classic polyamide
fibre
Width repeat
66.5cm (26⅛in)
Length repeat
95cm (37⅜in)
Manufacturer:
Vorwerk & Co.
Teppichwerke,
Germany

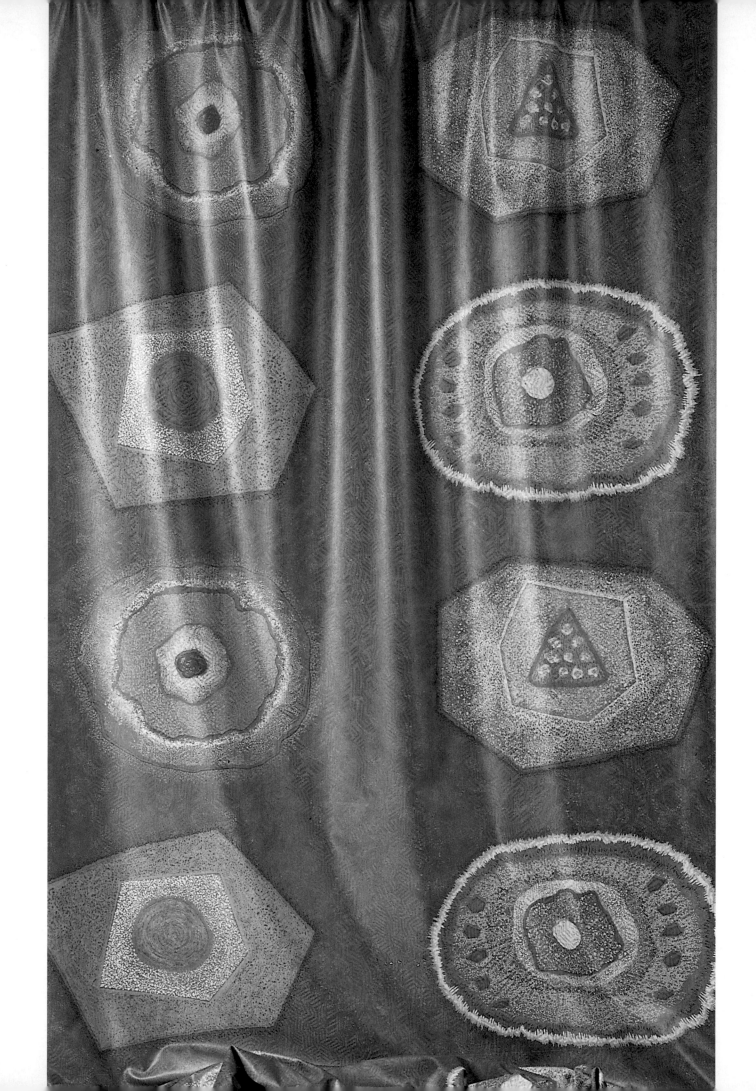

1. (Left) **Beppe Kessler**
Roncade
Screen-printed
curtain fabric
Cotton
Width repeat
90cm (35⅜in)
Length repeat
140cm (55in)
Manufacturer: Tanus
Textildruck Zimmer
GmbH and Co.,
Germany, for W.K.

Section
6

The Inner World

2. **Koji Hamai**
in collaboration with
Noboru Kolke
*Field Trip to a
Factory*
Installation, June
1994: 1,000 cotton
thread waste T-shirts

The term 'fibre art' until recently meant sculptures or wall-hangings, but the break-down of barriers means that functional textiles such as garments, scarves, quilts, fabrics and rugs are now also viewed as equally powerful means of conveying – and questioning – ideas. Both hand and machine made, the objects gathered together here demonstrate ways in which makers manipulate fibre, technique and colour to give substance to the invisible – philosophies, emotions or the meaning of textiles themselves.

Inspired by the 'intimate intensity of badges and stitched emblems, and by embroidery's history of story-telling', Tom Lundberg creates small pictures that encapsulate memories as well as glimpses of everyday life; also through embroidery, Tilleke Schwarz blends symbols of personal significance with references to the sampler tradition. Feliksas Jakubauskas weaves a response to Lithuanian folk textiles – namely the woven towels of natural and bleached linen – into 'Old Textile', while universal as well as personal symbols permeate Isabella Whitworth's resist and painted silks.

Speaking for many who choose to express themselves through textiles, Heather Allen describes cloth as 'a daily, tangible, tactile continuum within the experience of living'. Benoit Arsenault's response to life is captured as much by the swirling fury of colour, blockprinted on to silk scarves, as by their given title: 'The letter "A" as

in Arsenault and anarchist'. Reflecting on 'the enchanted circle of parent-child-bed with the wild night outside', Sarah Crowest's quilts carry images of charms, spells and rituals for safe passage; safety of a different sort was the goal for Eleanor Avery, using latex and human hair to exorcize her own inner conflicts by controlling human forms. For Koji Hamai, cloths are symbols of everyday living, and in 'Field Trip to a Factory' 1,000 T-shirts made from thread waste highlight the 'meaning of the special features of the fashion world – death and re-creation', but also express his concern for an industry with ageing workers who have no heirs to take their place.

Tapestry remains an important vehicle for self-expression, as shown by Aija Freimane and Ieva Krumina's emotionally saturated responses to Latvian folklore and ethnography. But often, the desire to give voice to inner vision has led to the evolution of individual methods of construction. Lisbeth Tolstrup, for example, combines fibres with metals and wood, and painted wood is woven with wool and linen into Sophie Pattinson's exuberant hangings.

3. (Left & above)
Heather Allen
Colour Library (and detail)
Reversible, hand-woven, painted, silk-screened rag rug
Limited batch production
Cotton, canvas, dyes, textile inks
Width
175.3cm (69in)
Height
228.6cm (90in)

4. (Right) **Isabella Whitworth**
Scarf on mythic studies
One-off
Habotai silk, twill, crêpe de Chine, Kniazeff dyes
Width 20.32cm (8in)
Height 137cm (54in)

5. (Left & right)
Sarah Crowest
Bedlam Spread
and *True Romance*
(details)
Direct-dyed and
screen-printed
fabric patchwork
One-off
Cottons, damask
backing, cotton
embroidery thread
Bedlam Spread (left):
Width
193cm (75⅞in)
Height
247cm (97¼in)
True Romance:
Width
172cm (67⅝in)
Height
222cm (87⅜in)

6. **Ieva Krumina**
Paradise Garden
Tapestry
One-off
Wool, cotton,
synthetics
Width
150cm (59in)
Height
200cm (78⅜in)

7. **Ieva Krumina**
Tree of Light
Tapestry
One-off
Wool, cotton,
synthetics
Width
100cm (39⅜in)
Height
150cm (59in)

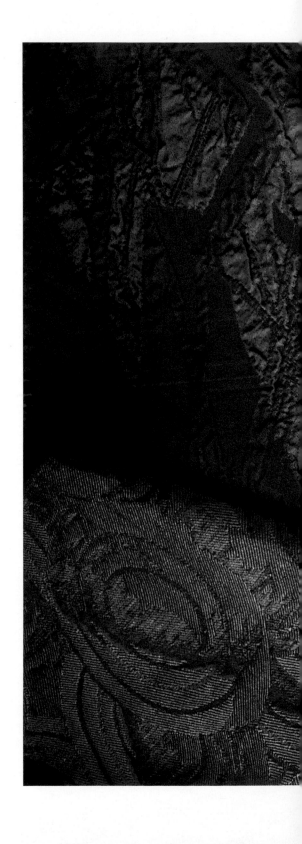

8. **Philippa Brock**
Discs Abstract 1
(with colourways)
CAD woven Jacquard
Limited batch production
Wool worsted warp,
viscose, Tactel chenille,
knop; worsted weft
Piece width 60 –122cm
24 – 48in)
Repeat 30.5cm x
30.5cm (12in x 12in)

8. **Philippa Brock**

10. **Eleanor Avery**
Eight Ate (detail)
One-off
Latex, human hair,
mixed media
Width
190cm (74¾in)
Height
138cm (54½in)

11. **Benoit Arsenault**
A
Hand-blockprinted
fabric
Limited batch
production
Silk twill
Piece width
20cm (7⅞in)
Piece length
150cm (59in)
Manufacturer:
Court Métrage,
Canada

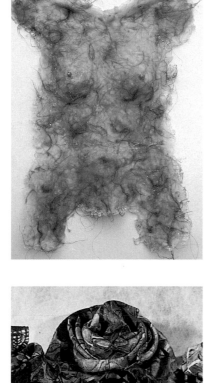

12. **Sophie Pattinson**
Textile Mobile
Handwoven
One-off
Wood, wool, linen
Width
61cm (24in)
Height
853.4cm (336in)

13. **Jan Truman**
Venus
One-off
Machine-knitted
wire, embroidery
threads, glass
beads, found
objects
Width 76cm (29⅞in)
Height 105cm (41⅓in)

9. (Left) **Kate Egan**
Houses on Sticks
Construction
One-off
Lino, fabric, stitch,
wood, metal
Width
105cm (41⅓in)
Height
200cm (78⅜in)

14. (Below and right)
Tom Lundberg
Decorative Touches
(and detail)
Hand and machine
embroidery
One-off
Cotton, rayon, silk,
metallic threads on
rayon velvet
Width
33cm (13in)
Height
33cm (13in)

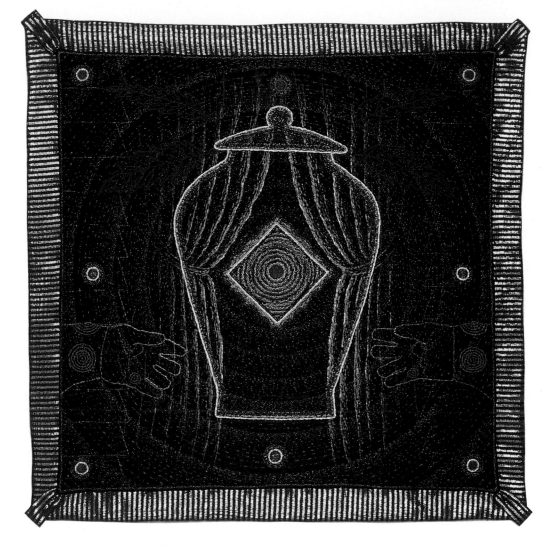

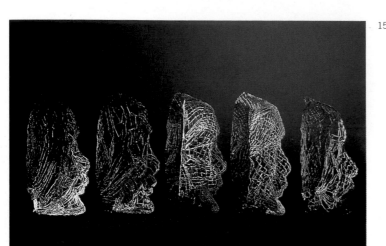

15. Teresa Pla
Masks
Moulded
sprang masks
One-off
Cotton
Width
35cm (13¾in)
Height
20cm (7⅞in)

16. **Lisbeth Tolstrup**
Traces of Textile
One-off, part of
series of 24
Copper, felt,
iron, slate, wool
Width 12cm (4⅝in)
Height 12cm (4⅝in)

17. (Right)
Tilleke Schwarz
*Beware of
Embroidery*
Embroidery on
dyed linen
One-off
Cotton, silk on
linen, textile
dye, paint
Width
55cm (21⅝in)
Height
60cm (23⅝in)

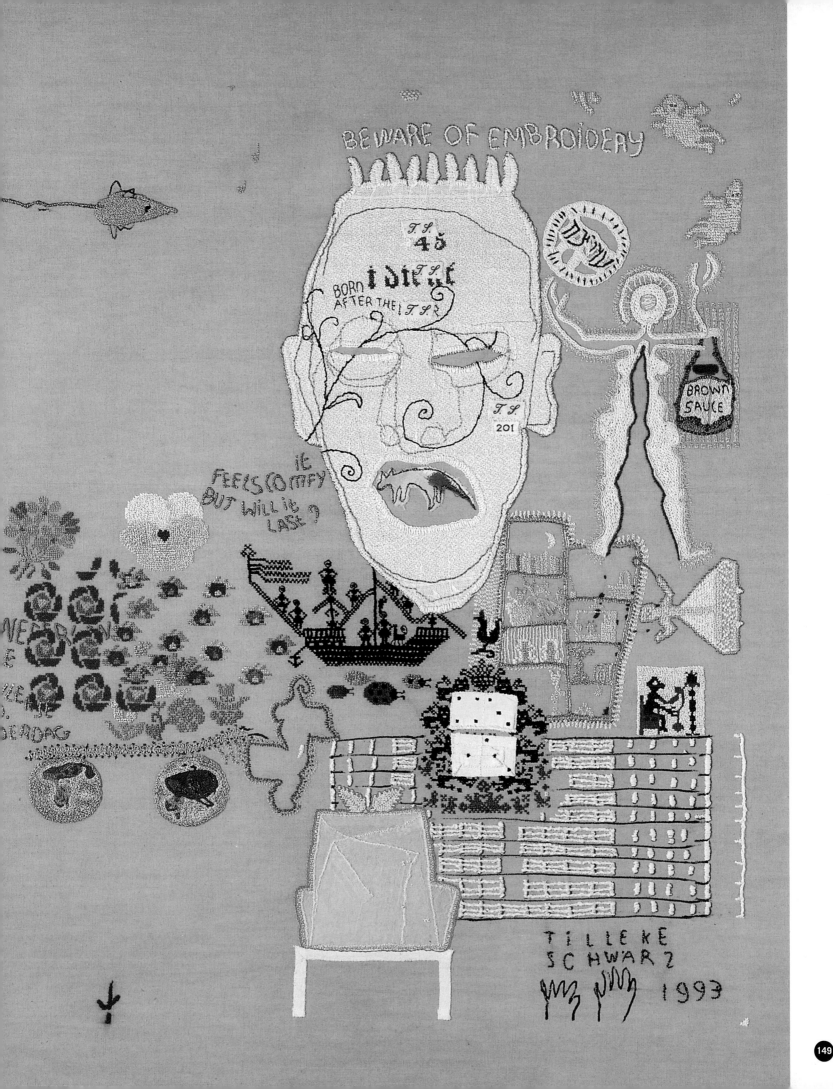

149

18. **Charlotte Hodge**
The Gazebo
Hand and machine-
stitched embroi-
dered textile collage
One-off
Silk, velvet, chiffon,
cotton, wool
Width
34cm (13⅜in)
Height
35cm (13¾in)

20. **Charlotte Hodge**
Hot shot (detail)
Hand and machine-
stitched embroidered
wall-hanging
One-off
Silk, velvet,
chiffon, wool
Width
112cm (44in)
Height
120cm (47⅛in)

19. **Lala de Dios**
Pagoda
Double-faced
handwoven rug
Limited batch
production
Cotton, wool
Width
130cm (51⅛in)
Height
195cm (76¾in)

22. **Kurt Meinecke**
    Design No. 11
    Handtufted rug
    Limited batch
    production
    Wool
    Width

    1.21m (4ft)
    Height
    1.83m (6ft)
    Manufacturer:
    Landin Products,
    Inc., USA

23. **Luciano Bartolini**
    Simian
    Handtufted rug
    Wool
    Width
    240cm (94½in)
    Height
    300cm (118in)
    Manufacturer:
    Driade SpA, Italy

21. (Left) **Helen Yardley**
    Siena
    Handtufted rug
    Pure new wool
    Width 180cm
    (70⅞in)
    Height 270cm
    (106¼in)
    Manufacturer:
    Toulemonde
    Bochart, France

24. **Anna Gerretz**
Untitled
Tapestry
One-off
Wool, linen, cotton
Width
310cm (122in)
Height
165cm (64⅞in)

25. **Feliksas Jakubauskas**
Old Textile
Tapestry
One-off
Wool, synthetic fibre
Width
128cm (50⅜in)
Height
115cm (45¼in)

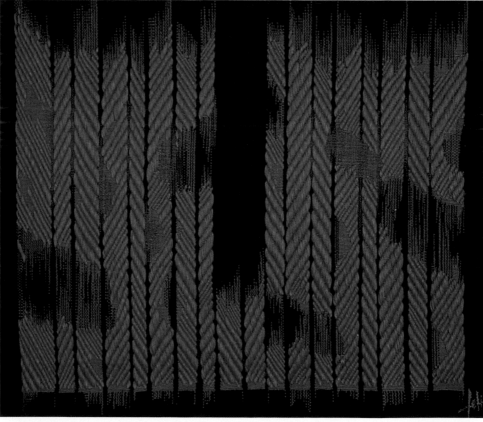

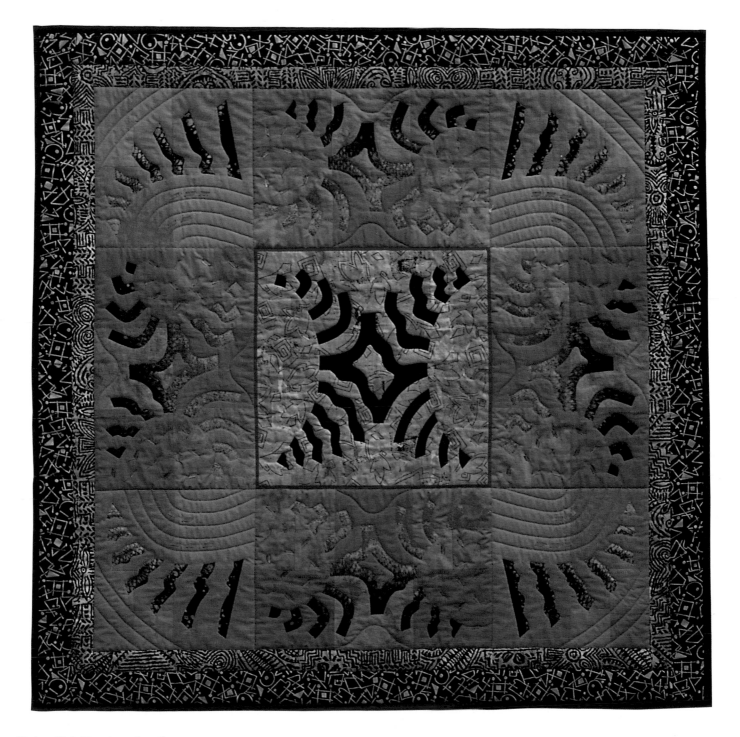

26. **Anne-Marie Stewart**   One-off
    Reverberations–Pink   Cotton
    Machine-quilted   Width 116cm
    and pieced,   (45⅝in)
    hand-appliqued   Height 116cm
    wall-hanging   (45⅝in)

28. (Right) **Hiroshi Awatsuji**
Michi
Screen print
Cotton
Width repeat
135cm (53⅛in)
Length repeat
180cm (70⅞in)
Manufacturer:
Design House
AWA, Japan

27. **Adriana Franco**
Chicle Bazooka
Industrial
carpeting collage
One-off
Linen, metal,
thermo-adhesive
bands
Width
213cm (83⅞in)
Height
117cm (46in)

Many works in this section are highly coloured, an acknowledgement of the powerful messages conveyed by intense hues. Colour is a natural starting point for **Adriana Franco**, a colourist for an architectural firm in Seville as well as for carpet manufacturers, Texart; Franco uses Texart's product to create rugs that break with traditional rug forms. **Helen Yardley** (page 153) also designs rugs, but for her colour and the creation of space, rather than form, are the fundamental considerations. In embroidery and quilt-making respectively, **Charlotte Hodge** (pages 150, 151) and **Anne-Marie Stewart** (page 155) celebrate the illusionary and expressive potential of colour, while on a machine-printed cotton **Hiroshi Awatsuji** blends reds to capture both majesty and peace.

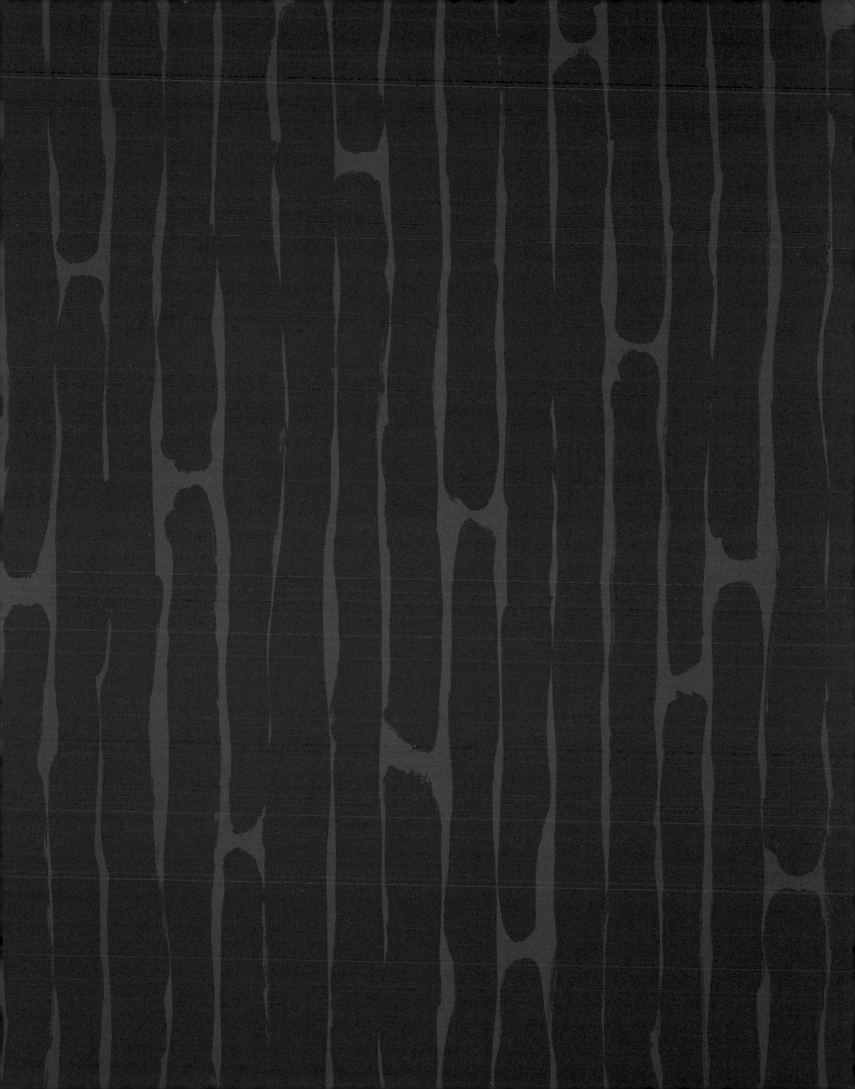

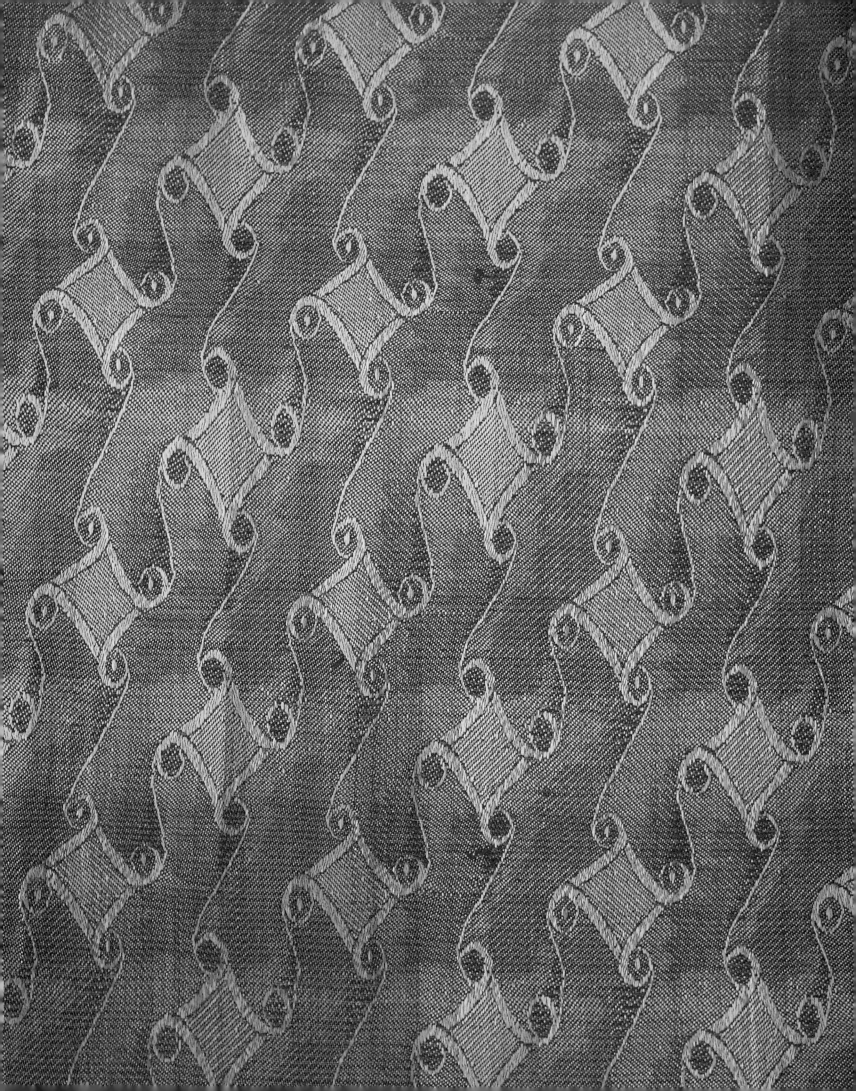

1. (Left) **Margarete Ilse Ritchie**
Winchester
Handwoven Jacquard
One-off
Silk warp; tussah
silk weft
Piece width
22cm (8⅝in)

Section ⑦ Young Designers

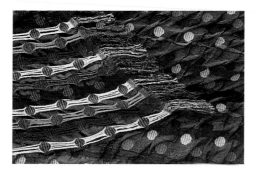

2. **Sarah Cole**
Spots and Stripes
Hand dobby-woven fabric
One-off
Botany wool, cotton
Piece width
86.4cm (34in)
Piece length
200cm (78⅞in)

Young designers in this instance refers to those who, irrespective of age, have completed their training within the last two years, or who are still students. This was not taken into account during the selection. In fact, if placed in the previous chapters, there would be nothing to distinguish the work of established professionals from that of these young designers. The reason for presenting young designers as a separate group is to provide a special focus on the talents emerging from textile courses around the world.

A sample of second-year Bachelor of Arts Textile Design work from the Royal Melbourne Institute of Technology highlights the serious pursuit of ecologically sound textiles. In a project co-ordinated by Senior Lecturer Patrick Snelling, the students were required to create a book of swatches using only natural fabrics and fibres, natural dyeing or colouring agents. The emphasis was on decorating surfaces without using photo-chemicals, looms or double-bed powered machinery, although a sewing machine was permissible to speed up the making process; construction was designed to exaggerate the inherent qualities of the materials.

From Canada come hand screen direct and discharge printed examples created in the studio-workshops of Le centre de recherche et de design en impression textile de Montréal. Founded in l985 by Robert Lamarre and Monique Beauregard

to provide working space, resources and a forum for professional surface and printed textile designers, the centre offered its first three-year degree course, with Cegap du Vieux-Montréal, in 1989. Students work side-by-side with the professionals, and the outcome of this 'real world' environment is highlighted by the juxtaposition of work by Beauregard and student Johanne Ducharme.

A group of batiks from The Latvian Academy of Art demonstrate the emotional power of this medium: one work by Aija Freimane expresses 'future through the pain', while another by Rizijs Marians 'tells about [the] fickleness and fragility of time'.

Exploration of a wide range of materials is characteristic of the work of British students, including Lucie Hernandez and Tania Johnson, both of whom incorporate wire into their work, with very different results. Feathers find their place in latex bonded textiles by Suzanne Duffy, and, entrapped with nails in gauzes by Rachel Pearson, they evoke the 'sharp and soft' contradiction of birds. Linda Chorostecki incorporates heat-sealed pictures with pigment and discharge printing to create customized nostalgic collaged cloths, while Sharon Smith uses hand-knotted chenille to increase the delicacy of contrast between painted organza and Cornely embroidery. Exploiting the way in which fibres burn, Sue Hartree creates extremes of subtlety.

4. **Johano Boden Spiers**
Untitled fabric design
Collage
One-off
Paper (book pages,
postage stamps)
Width
33cm (13in)
Height
45.7cm (18in)

5. **Rebecca Chivers**
Seaweed Length
Hand dobby-woven
One-off
700 denier
monofilament nylon,
cotton warp; high-
twist wool weft
Piece width
91.4cm (36in)
Piece length
914.4cm (360in)

The constructed textiles course led by Gary Rooney at Winchester School of Art, England, promotes creative design with a sound technical base, catering both to Bachelor of Arts and Master of Arts students. Combining the study of fabric construction with dye, print and finishing techniques produces innovative prototypes, ranging from **Jill Myerscough**'s embroidered and dyed knits to **Rebecca Vaile**'s knitwear, with dyed and printed dresses and felted coats. This approach also allows for the development of new 'document' fabrics: **Margarete Ilse Ritchie**'s dyed silk and tussah Jacquard weave (page 158) interprets a plaster ceiling at Dorset House in England, and although developed on a computer, was woven by hand.

3. (Top left)
Rebecca Vaile
RV
Machine-knitted,
discharged dyed,
printed dress;
machine knitted
and felted coat
Limited batch
production
Dress: viscose
Coat: Lurex wire, wool
Made to measure

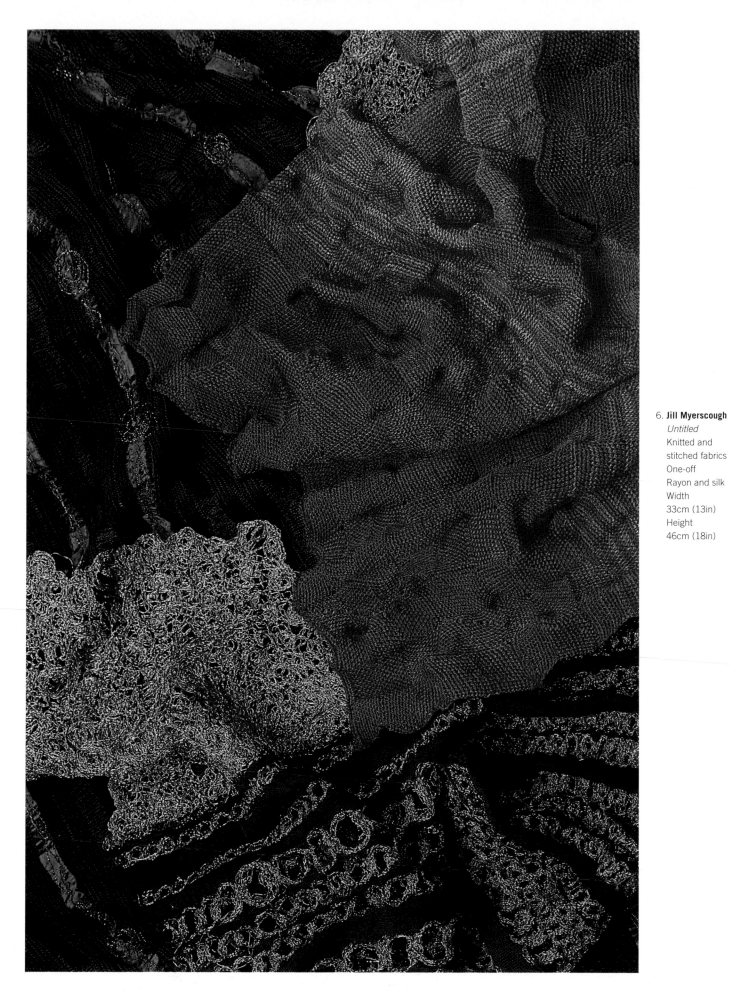

6. **Jill Myerscough**
Untitled
Knitted and
stitched fabrics
One-off
Rayon and silk
Width
33cm (13in)
Height
46cm (18in)

8. **Monique Beauregard**
Graffiti II
Hand screen prints
with discharged and
illuminating colours
Limited batch
production
Cotton sateen
Width repeat
135cm (53⅛in)
Length repeat
45cm (17⅝in)

9. **Louise Kilner**
Untitled
Dip-dyed, sprayed
and discharged
screen print
One-off
Silk chiffon,
Procion dyes
Width repeat
120cm (47¼in)
Length repeat
68.3cm (26⅞in)

10. **Rizijs Marians**
*Sand-Glass and
Other Things*
Batik
One-off
Cotton
Width
120cm (47¼in)
Height
160cm (63in)

7. (Left) **Johanne Ducharme**
Lumières
Hand-painted,
hand screen
print
Limited batch
production
Cotton velvet
Piece width
140cm (55in)

Piece length
140cm (55in)
Width repeat
140cm (55in)
Length repeat
180cm (70⅞in)
Manufacturer:
Centre de recherche
et de design en
impression textile de
Montréal, Canada

(Below)
Hand-knitted
cotton fibre

12. (Right) **Melanie
Abraham**
Pineapple
Hand leno-woven
and felted fabric
One-off
Lambswool,
monofilament
Piece width
61cm (24in)
Piece length
228.6cm (90in)
Width repeat
10.2cm (4in)
Length repeat
10.2cm (4in)

(Below)
Stitched and burnt
cotton calico

11. **Royal Melbourne
Institute of Technology**
*BA Textile Design
Students*
Eco Fabrics (details)
Piece widths
42cm (16½in)
Piece lengths
30cm (11¾in)

(Above)
Crocheted cotton,
dyed with beetroot

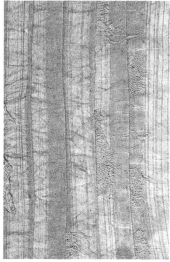

(Above)
Pleated cotton and
raw silk, dyed with
waste vegetable pulp

14. **Hilary Windridge**
Eggfall
Hand print
One-off
Silk crêpe de
Chine, Procion and
mineral dyes
Piece width
38cm (15in)
Piece length
38cm (15in)

13. **Rachel-Ann Muncaster**
Untitled
Hand-knitted
scarves (detail)
One-off
Wool/lycra mix,
rayon, combed
cotton, Lurex, fancy
bouclé, black
bin liners
Piece width
50cm (19⅝in)
Piece length
150cm (59in)

15. **Suzanne Duffy**
Embossed Fern
Plaster moulded
construction from
design plate
Prototype
Latex and pigment
Width
43cm (17in)
Height
106.7cm (42in)

16. **Karen Ferguson**
Meridian
Hand silk-screen and
discharged print
Limited batch production
Velvet, direct dyes
Piece width
160cm (63in)
Piece length
200cm (78⅝in)

17. **Brenda Connor**
Cranes of Bharatpur
Handpainted and
stitched construction
One-off
Handmade paper,
metallic threads,
beads, spangles,
metallic powders,
goldfinger and
liquid pearl
Width 68cm (26¾in)
Height 56cm (22in)

18. (Below, left & right)
Martin McShane
Blue/Black Circle
(and reverse, left)
Double-sided bonded,
hand-cut macramé
construction

One-off
Cotton velvet,
polyester crêpe
Width
60cm (23⅝in)
Height
60cm (23⅝in)

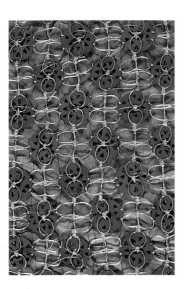

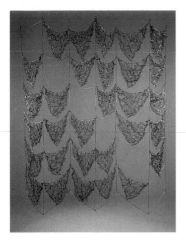

19. **Lucie Hernandez**
Geometric Piece
Knitted construction
One-off
Electric wire,
brazing rods
Width
232cm (91⅛in)
Height
180cm (70⅞in)

21 **Karen Smith**
Life after Decay
(and detail, right)
Construction
One-off
Recycled fabric
and paper,
mixed media
Width
25cm (9¾in)
Height
38cm (15in)

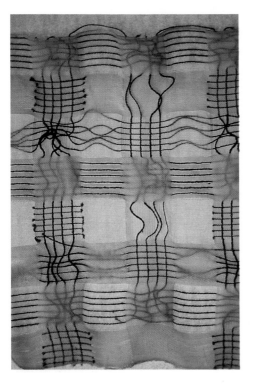

20. **Tania Johnson**
Disorder and Simplicity
Handwoven fabric
One-off
Polyamide, cotton,
nylon, transparent
sewing thread
Piece width
16.5cm (6½in)
Piece length
16.5cm (6½in)
Width repeat
6.4cm (2½in)
Length repeat
9cm (3½in)

22. **Tara Hansford**
Bound Interaction
Construction
One-off
Wood, metals,
cotton fabrics,
string
Repeat
5cm (2in)

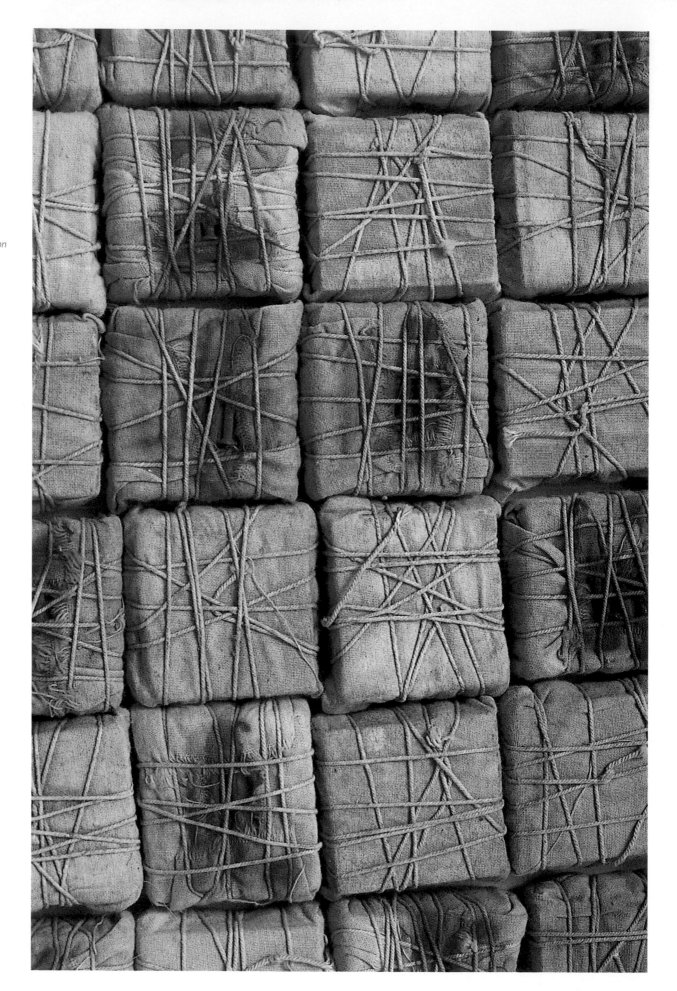

23. **Alexandra Eton**
G
Double-faced,
discharge-printed
and devoré cloth
One-off
Suedette, dyes
Piece width
106.7cm (42in)
Piece length
137.2cm (54in)

24. **Fiona Hely-Hutchinson**
Aboriginal Dream II
Pin-board and loom-
woven hanging
One-off
Cotton warp;
wool weft
Width
175.2cm (69in)
Height
233.7cm (92in)

25. **Aija Freimane**
Pink Dream Cow I
Cold-resist batik
Prototype
Nylon, synthetic dyes
Width
105cm (41⅛in)
Height
76cm (29⅞in)

26. **Aija Freimane**
Cat's Stroke III
Cold-resist batik
Prototype
Nylon, synthetic
dyes
Width
70cm (27½in)
Height
76cm (29⅞in)

27. **Linda Chorostecki**
Who is Mary Broadbent?
Hand-printed repro-
mastered photographs,
heatsealed colour
photocopies
One-off
Cotton satin, discharge
dyes, pigments
Width 52cm (20½in)
Height 300cm (118in)

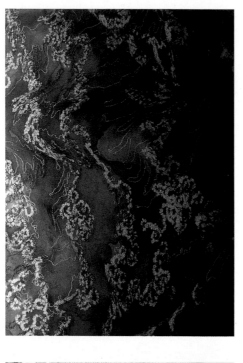

28. Sharon Smith
Untitled
Handpainted and
hand-stitched fabric
with attached hand-
knotted chenille
One-off
Silk organza,
silk paints,
chenille, rayon
Piece width
113cm (44½in)
Piece length
193cm (75⅞in)

29. Sharon Smith
Untitled
Cornely machine
and hand-stitched,
handpainted fabric
One-off
Polyester chiffon,
silk paints, rayon
Piece width
76cm (29⅞in)
Piece length
185.5cm (73in)

30. Rachel Pearson
Untitled
Nylon net
One-off
Upholsterers' tacks,
cockerel tail feathers
affixed with PVC
wood glue
Piece width
183cm (72in)
Piece length
364cm (143¼in)

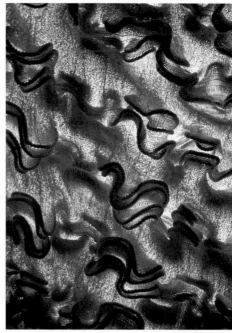

31. Anne Hübel
Stretch under Stress
Sewing machine,
appliqué embroidery
Prototype
Cotton fabric,
packaging ribbon
Piece width
40cm (15¾in)
Piece length
50cm (19⅝in)
Manufacturer:
ZSK, Zangs Stickerei
Krefeld, Germany

32. (Right)
Sue Hartree
Untitled
Hand-dobby
doubleweave,
burnt
One-off
Spun tussah
and filament
silk, cotton
Piece width
71cm (28in)
Piece length
244cm (96in)

● Designers

Helle Abild was born in Copenhagen, Denmark, in 1964 and graduated in textile design in 1989. A freelance textile designer, she has also designed furniture, including a sales counter for the Royal Theatre in Copenhagen. She has worked in London and since 1993 has worked for the designer Jhane Barnes in New York. 3.30

Melanie Abraham studied at Winchester School of Art from 1989–90 and has just completed a BA degree course in Design in Woven Textiles at Chelsea College of Art and Design. In 1993 she was awarded 3rd prize at Surtex Bedscapes and her work was exhibited at Surtex, New York. In 1994 her work was selected for Texprint and exhibited at Interstoff, Frankfurt, Germany. 7.12

Luis Omar Acosta was born in Córdoba, Argentina in 1952 but studied at the Gerrit Rietveld Academy in Amsterdam, The Netherlands. Today he is a textile artist, specializing in tapestries and woven fabrics. He also designs fashion accessories, is the Dutch correspondent for Spanish and Argentinean magazines on textiles and teaches courses on 'Design for Woven Fabrics'. Notable exhibitions include solo shows at the Casa de España, Utrecht, and the Stadsmuseum, Woerden, The Netherlands. His work has appeared in group exhibitions at the Design Centre, Stuttgart, the International Textile Fair, Frankfurt, Germany; Academie Polimoda, Prato, Italy; the Municipal Museum of Art, Kyoto, Japan; and the Galerie Artfull Facilities, Amsterdam. 2.12

Razia Ahmed specializes in textiles and jewellery. In 1964–5 she studied textile design and printmaking at the Bournville School of Art, Birmingham, and has since spent extensive periods of time in the Far East studying batik and Ikat, in Sindh studying Pakistani textiles and in Egypt studying Islamic design. In 1989 she received a BA degree in Anthropology and Fine Art from the University of British Columbia, Canada. She has continued her studies by taking a Diploma in ceramics, photography and silkscreen printing and has recently completed a Master's degree in Social Anthropology. Throughout this period of extensive study Razia Ahmed has held various posts, including that of Museum Assistant at the Museum of Anthropology, University of British Columbia. Today she is a greetings

card and stationery designer for Collaboration International. Razia has exhibited her work widely and in 1986 held textile design workshops with Narkku Piri and Philip Werner at the Banff School of Fine Arts, Canada. 1.15

Heather Allen studied languages at the Nanzan University, Japan, before continuing her education in the USA, first with a BFA degree in painting and sculpture with a subsidiary in Japanese at the University of New Hampshire, and later at the University of Massachusetts where she trained in Artisanry–Fibres. She has exhibited her work widely within the USA, recently at the Crafts National 28, Pennsylvania, and at the Fantastic Fibers Show at the Yeiser Art Centre, Paducah, Kentucky. Heather Allen has lectured throughout the USA and since 1993 has held a Residency at the Appalachian Centre for Crafts in Smithville, Tennessee. 6.3

Junichi Arai was born in Kiryu, Gunma, Japan in 1932. Since the mid 1950s he has developed new techniques for weaving with metallic fibres and was given the Japanese International Trade Industry Minister's award in the Grand Fair of Synthetic Fibres in Japan in 1961. Arai works with both Japanese and international fashion designers and has exhibited internationally, most recently in the 'Textiles of the World' show at the Saint Louis Art Museum, USA. His work can be seen in the permanent collections of the Fashion Institute of Technology, USA; the Victoria & Albert Museum, London; the Museum of Art, Rhode Island School of Design, USA; the Cooper-Hewitt Museum, USA and the Okawa Museum, Kiryu, Japan. In 1987 Arai was awarded honorary membership of the British Royal Designers for Industry. 2.19

Xano Armenter (see Marieta Textiles)

Gertrud Arndt was born in Ratibor, Upper Silesia, in 1903. She studied at the Erfurt School of Arts and Crafts, and at the Bauhaus weaving workshop in Weimar under Georg Muche and in Dessau under Gunta Stölzl. She also took basic courses with Moholy-Nagy, Klee, Kandinsky and Adolf Meyer. She was awarded a Diploma on completion of her studies in 1927. 5.30

Maryke Arp is a designer of textile objects and is registered as such with the Cultural Council of South Holland, The Netherlands. She has exhibited her work frequently within her own country and also in Germany, Hungary and Switzerland. In 1994 she exhibited at the Miniartextil Biennal in Como, Italy. 2.22

Benoit Arsenault was born in Bonaventure, Quebec, Canada, in 1957 and has a BA in Fine Arts from the Université du Québec in Montreal. He went on to study textiles at the CRDITM and in 1994, with a fellow student, Isabelle Martin, started a small design and handprinting company called Court Métrage. The company designs and produces printed textiles for fashion and home furnishings. 6.13

Eleanor Avery obtained a BA degree in Multi-Media Textiles from Loughborough College of Art and Design. From 1992–3 she was a part-time lecturer at the North Warwickshire College, Nuneaton, UK. 6.11

Hiroshi Awatsuji was born in Kyoto, Japan, in 1929 and graduated from the Kyoto City University of Art. In 1964 he began his collaboration with the Fujie Textile Co. Ltd, and in 1988 he became a professor at the Tama University of Arts. He has participated in exhibitions throughout the world and is internationally recognized for his work. Awatsuji received an Outstanding Award at the 3rd International Textile Competition in Kyoto in 1992 and later that year a Gold Award at the 38th ID Annual Design Review in the USA. 4.6, 6.28

G. P. & J. Baker, which incorporates the fabric companies Parkertex and Fardis, was founded in 1884 by two brothers who had been strongly influenced by family visits to Turkey and oriental textile prints. They started by importing carpets and later having the textiles they had collected adapted into printed furnishing fabrics. The family business was bought by the textile division of Parker Knoll in the 1960s and in 1984 Baker celebrated its centenary with a five-month exhibition of its textiles at the Victoria & Albert Museum. Today the company employs over 100 people, designing and selling products throughout the UK, Europe, America, the Far East and Australasia. They offer a wide selection of fine printed, plain and woven furnishing fabrics and wallpapers, many based on archive designs. The last two years, however, have seen a refocusing of the G. P. & J. Baker range with the inclusion of a number of contemporary prints. 1.5, 5.26

Luciano Bartolini was born in Fiesole, Italy, in 1948. In his early work dating from 1973–4 he mostly used packing material, and he won much acclaim for his Kleenex series which he exhibited in numerous group shows including the XIV Biennial of Contemporary Art in Sao Paulo, as well as one-man shows in Italy and Germany. In 1983 he won a study grant from DAAD in Berlin where he lived for a year. He has continued to exhibit his work throughout Europe. 6.23

Monique Beauregard was born in Montreal, Canada, in 1945. She has undergone extensive training in art and design, researching textile design at Goldsmiths' College, London from 1972–3 and computer-aided textile design in 1986. In 1986 she also conducted a survey of the art and design education system in Great Britain. Most recently she has been studying ancient printing methods in France and England. Since 1974 Monique Beauregard has worked for Séri in Montreal as textile designer and associate. During this time she has held various educational positions, including a consultancy for a programme development in textile design and printing for the Ministries of Education and Manpower, Quebec. In 1985, along with Robert Lamarre, she co-founded the Centre de recherche et de design en impression textile de Montréal. She has exhibited her work in Canada, USA and Europe, notably at the Grand Prix des Métiers d'Art 'The Americas' in Montreal, an exhibition which also toured in North America. 7.8

Monica Bella-Broner was born in Nuremberg, Germany, in 1911 as Monica Ullmann. She studied under Gunta Stölzl at the Bauhaus weaving workshop in Dessau (having taken a foundation course under Josef Albers, and studied colour theory and analytical drawing with Klee and Kandinsky). In 1937 she emigrated to Palestine, opening her own workshop with Arieh Sharon, and the following year moved to Los Angeles, USA, where she had her own studio for production design and set decoration. In the late 1940s she spent a couple of years in Paris before returning to the USA to work as a textile stylist in the industry. From 1968 to her death in 1993 she lived and worked in Stuttgart. 5.28

Kristine Birzniece is a textile artist who lives and works in Latvia. She studied at the Latvian Art Academy. 1.28

Jehane Boden Spiers studied at Eastbourne College of Art and Technology, the Winchester School of Art, UK, and the Reutlingen Fachhochschule für Technik und Wirtschaft, Germany. She has a BA Honours degree in Printed Textiles and has written a thesis entitled 'Automated Artists – William Latham'. She has exhibited in London and Brighton and her work has been sold through various outlets including Gallery Five (wrapping paper and greetings cards) and Liberty of London (handmade limited edition embroidered books). She also designs textiles for fashion and furnishings. 7.4

Eta Sadar Breznik was born in Ljubljana, Slovenia, and graduated from the University of Architecture there in 1976. Today she works as a freelance textile designer.2.8

Philippa Brock received a BA Honours degree in textiles from Goldsmiths' College, London, in 1991, followed by an MA from the Royal College of Art. Since 1991 she has been a freelance designer of innovative woven fabrics. Recent commissions include a fashion marketing range for

the Lurexco Spring/Summer '96 collection and for the Safilin-France Spring/Summer '96 and Autumn/Winter collections. She has exhibited her work internationally. In 1994 she became a research fellow in CAD woven Jacquard design at Winchester School of Art. 6.8

Iben Brøndum was born in 1958 and educated at the College of Arts and Crafts in Copenhagen, Denmark. His work can be seen in public collections within Denmark, including the Danish National Museum of Decorative Arts. In 1992 he held a solo exhibition at the Museum of Contemporary Art in Roskilde, Denmark. 2.11

Bozena Burgielska studied in the Faculty of Artistic Fabric at the Higher School of Arts in Lodz, Poland. She is currently both Manager of the Design Department and Principal Designer of the Kowary Carpet Factory. She is a prize-winner of many arts competitions and is the laureate of the commercial fabric category of the International Triennale in Lodz. Her carpets are exhibited internationally, notably at the Hanover Domotex Annual Fair, Germany, and sell in the UK, Ireland, Middle East, Japan and Australia. She is often commissioned by established carpet manufacturers throughout the world to create exclusive designs for their collections. 5.19

Penny Carey Wells graduated from the Tasmanian School of Art in 1970, after which she taught art until 1983 while undertaking postgraduate study into drawing and papermaking techniques. She was made an Honorary Research Associate at the University of Tasmania in 1984 and today is a part-time lecturer and technician in paper-making at the University of Tasmania. Penny Carey Wells has exhibited her work extensively in Australia and is visiting lecturer at the Canberra School of Art, University of Canberra. She has lectured in the art of papermaking in Japan, the Philippines, the USA and The Netherlands. 3.2, 25

Karin Carlander was born in 1959. She worked at the Jette Nevers Workshop from 1980–82 before enrolling at the Textile Department of the Danish School of Art and Design. She graduated in 1987 and today is a member of the Design Group OCTO. 4.24

Rebecca Chivers graduated from Winchester School of Art, UK, in June 1993 and obtained a place with Texprint for the 1993 show Interstoff in Frankfurt. She is currently designing samples to specific briefs for a selling agency, Nicky, and since September 1994 has been undertaking an MA at Central Saint Martin's College of Art and Design, London. 7.5

Linda Chorostecki completed a BTEC National Diploma in Surface Pattern Design at the Jacob Kramer College in Leeds, and a BA Honours degree in Art and Design at Bretton Hall College in Wakefield. She is currently undertaking a postgraduate degree in Curriculum Education at Bretton Hall College and is a freelance designer. 7.27

Sarah Cole studied at the Falmouth School of Art and Design, UK, followed by the Winchester School of Art (BA Honours degree in Woven Textiles) and the Royal College of Art (MA in Woven Textiles). Since 1992 she has sold work through an agent, conducted trade show research for Premiere Vision, Paris, undertaken a cloth finishing course in Bradford and worked as Assistant to the Designer for IMTA, Desii Mode, Italy working on classic woven textiles for apparel. She has exhibited her work in young designers shows and in 1993/94 was awarded a scholarship from the Textile Institute. 7.2

Liza Collins was born in London in 1961. She trained at the North East London Polytechnic, graduating with a BA

Honours degree in Fine Art. Her solo exhibitions include 'Tapestries and Paintings' at Camden Arts Centre(1989); and two shows for the Barbican Centre, London, 'Prints and Decorated Glass' (1993) and 'Small Tapestries and Prints' (1994). She has many private clients, and work in corporate collections includes designs for McDonald Hamburgers Ltd, The Contemporary Arts Society, the Victoria and Albert Museum and the Epping Forest District Museum, Essex. 1.17

Brenda Connor is a member of the Embroiderers' Guild and a founder member of the Cheshire Textile Group, of which she has been group secretary and was the first exhibition organizer. She has exhibited her work at locations throughout the UK and her work has featured on the cover of *Embroidery* magazine. She has also written for the magazine on the subject of embroidered paper. 7.17

Courtaulds is an international chemical company covering the areas of polymer technology, surface science and cellulose chemistry in all activities from coatings, sealants and adhesives to aerospace composites, flooring, packaging, chemicals, fibres and films. The origins of Courtaulds can be traced to the late 1600s when the Courtauld family arrived in England as Huguenot refugees. In 1816 Samuel Courtauld III started his own silk-weaving business. The company's origins in man-made fibres go back to the beginning of this century when the viscose rayon business was established. Acetate yarns and fibres followed during the 1920s and Courtelle acrylic fibre in the 1950s. These three fibres still form the core of Courtaulds' fibre business and have recently been joined by Tencel. Page 7

Lena Cronholm has worked for Borås Cotton AB, Sweden since 1976, specializing in bed linen and haberdashery. 1.8

Gloria Crouse studied at the University of Washington, USA, undertaking postgraduate studies in metals/welding and architecture. She has exhibited widely in the USA and her work has been collected by some of the leading corporate concerns in Washington. Examples of her designs can be found in the Tacoma Art Museum, Tacoma, Washington. 3.28, 29

Sarah Crowest works in dyed and screen-printed textiles, mosaic and screen-printed ceramics. She studied clothing design and textile printing at Medway College of Design, Kent, and textile design at Middlesex Polytechnic. In 1985 she emigrated to Australia, where she worked for various textile companies before forming her own studio at the Jam Factory and Design Centre, Adelaide, in 1992. She has held many shows within Australia and in 1993 developed a range of screen-printed bags and ceramics which she took on exhibition to Okayama, Japan. Sarah Crowest's work can be seen in the permanent collection of the Powerhouse Museum, Sydney, and the Stanthorpe Art Gallery, Queensland and she is a member of the Crafts Council of South Australia and the Experimental Art Foundation. In 1993 she was awarded an Art for Public Places Grant for the collaborative environmental temporary art project ' A Fish Affair'. 6.5

Anne Crowther studied Textile Design at Central Saint Martin's, London, graduating with a specialization in woven textiles. With the aid of the Yorkshire and Humberside Art Grants she set up in business and continues to create new work at her studio in Bradford. She has frequently exhibited her work in the UK. 1.23

Dédar was born in 1970 and now works in the family textile studio, designing upholstery fabrics and sheers. He has already received international acclaim for his fabrics. 5.9

Lala de Dios was born in Corunna, Spain. She obtained a degree in the History of Art from Madrid Complutense University, after which she worked as a teacher for several years. From 1977–8, following a grant from the Spanish Ministry of Industry, she studied handweaving with foot-powered looms at the Main School of Crafts in Madrid. In the early 1980s she opened a textile workshop in Madrid, where she taught and produced handwoven articles. At the same time she continued to study, most notably with the French artist Jacqueline Trubert in 1982 and in England at West Surrey College of Art and Design where she undertook a summer course in textile design in 1984. Lala de Dios exhibits her work in Spain and Portugal and frequently lectures on topics related to textile crafts and history. She has been instrumental in the establishment of textile craft cooperatives in rural areas as well as in the setting up of curricular textile activities in private and public schools for the disabled and in adult education. She is a founder member of the Asociación de Creadores Textiles de Madrid of which she was chairwoman during the period 1988–92. 6.19

Françoise Dorget started her professional career as director of contemporary interior design for the antique dealers Didier Aaron and Alain Demachy. In 1974 she opened her own studio, Etamine, in Paris, France, and in 1980 developed a line of fabrics and wallpapers. She has now created hew own consultancy firm dedicated to the home, Françoise Dorget Companie, and has opened shops in Paris, Toulouse and Lyons. 1.9

Johanne Ducharme was born in 1949 in Cabano, Quebec, Canada. She studied Fine Arts at the École des Beaux-Arts and has worked as a costume designer with dance companies in Montreal. In 1992 she decided to study Textile Design and Print at CRDITM, where she is still a student. 7.7

Suzanne Duffy graduated from Loughborough College of Art and Design with a BA Honours degree in Multi-Media Textiles in 1994. As winner of the RSA Student Design Awards – Innovative Fashion Fabrics – she was the recipient of a travel bursary in 1994 and was also selected to exhibit at the New Designers show, London, as well as at the Design Museum, London. She was involved with costume construction for the Demarco European Art Foundation and Jane Frere at the Edinburgh Arts Festival in 1994 and has also taken part in the Indigo Trade Fair, Paris. Her work has been published in Elle Decoration, the Vidal Sassoon pilot magazine and the Manchester Evening News. 7.15

Christie Dunning studied art and business administration before attending the San Diego State University, USA, where she obtained an MFA in Art. She is a member of California Fibres, and the Southern California representative of the Surface Design Association. She lectures at weavers guild meetings and has exhibited her work widely within the USA, including a solo exhibition in 1993, 'Heart, Mind and Soul: Seeking Security', at the Everett Gee Jackson Gallery, San Diego University. 4.13

E.I. Du Pont de Nemours & Co. was founded in 1802 in the USA and is today among the world's 20 largest industrial corporations. Its main businesses are in the areas of man-made fibres, polymer products, agricultural and industrial chemicals, industrial and consumer products, biomedical products, and petroleum and gas exploration, production, refining and marketing. The company is the inventor of Teflon and Lycra. Page 8

Jilly Edwards was born in 1948 and studied at the West of England College of Art and Edinburgh College of Art. Her work has been exhibited extensively within the UK and she has twice been awarded the Northern Arts Artists Awards (1993, 1994). Her designs, which are a personal response to landscape, have been acquired by the Architectural firm Ahrends, Burton and Koralek and through their offices have been shown in the UK, USA, Europe, Canada and Australia. 1.10

Kate Egan is an artist based in Manchester, UK, who designs and constructs large-scale interior and exterior textiles for public buildings and recreational spaces. She has recently been awarded a Crafts Council Setting-up Grant and is currently working on a large textile installation to celebrate the opening of a new textiles venue at Manchester Metropolitan University. 6.9

Ingrid Enarsson was born in Sweden in 1945. She has shown her work at numerous exhibitions, including the 1st International Fibre Art Symposium at Alden Biesen, Belgium, and at the 5th International Symposium of Textiles at Ruzumberok, Slovakia. She has worked on public commissions for hotels, office buildings, concert halls and hospitals, and has work in private collections. From 1987–8 she studied at the Academy of Fine Arts, Warsaw, Poland. 4.22, 23

Alexandra Eton took a BA Honours degree in Design at Chelsea College of Art and Design and is currently working for an MA in Fashion Textiles at the Central Saint Martin's College of Art and Design. She has received two RSA bursaries, and awards from the Clothworkers' Foundation, the Philological Foundation, Acton Charities and the Academy of Young Jewish Artists. She has exhibited her work at Indigo in Paris, New Designers and Decorex 1993. 7.23

Karen Ferguson studied at Glasgow School of Art, receiving a BA Honours degree in Printed and Knitted Textiles in 1994. She has received an Innovation Award for Textile Design from the Weavers' Guild and was sponsored by the Embroiderers' Guild to display at the Knitting and Stitching Show in 1994. She has designed stage costumes for several productions, most notably The Magic Flute performed at the Tramway, Glasgow, for which she was also responsible for the set design and stage management. She has exhibited at the New Designers Show, London, the National Gallery, and Edinburgh Artists and Artists Craftsmen. She recently set up her own studio, called Textiles to Commission. 7.16

Anne Field has been weaving and spinning since 1962. She was self taught before beginning her studies at Canterbury University, New Zealand, in 1983 and is presently completing a BA in Education and Art History. She has taught in New Zealand and in 1981 was invited to lecture at the First Australian Fibre Conference. Since then she has taught at many workshops in Canada, the USA, UK and Europe, including the Threads and Convergence conferences in England in 1990. She has exhibited her work in her native New Zealand and internationally at selected venues. 4.25

Kitty Fischer was born in 1908 as Catherine Louise van der Mijll Dekker. From 1929–32 she studied under Gunta Stölzl in the Bauhaus weaving workshop at Dessau (following the foundation course under Josef Albers, studying the theory of forms and analytical drawings under Kandinsky, and further courses under Joost Schmidt and Paul Klee), receiving a Diploma signed by Mies van der Rohe. She moved to Nunspeet in The Netherlands and founded her own studio, later working with Greten Köhler and Hermann Fischer. In 1933 she took part in the Triennale di Milano where she received a silver medal for two cellophane

materials. She worked on commissions for public buildings and museums and designs for the Dutch textile industry and later the Dutch Royal Family. In 1935 she participated in the Dutch entry for the World Exhibition in Brussels, where she was awarded the Gold Medal; and in the World's Fair in Paris, where she received the Diplôme d'Honneur. From 1934–79 Kitty Fischer was the weaving instructor at Amsterdam's Arts and Crafts School. 5.29

Sally Fox studied entomology at California Polytechnic State University at San Luis Obispo. She became interested in pest control following a study trip to the Gambia, and in 1982 received a graduate degree in Integrated Pest Management from the University of California at Riverside. She was introduced to coloured cotton in the 1980s while working for a cotton breeder whose focus was developing pest resistant strains of cotton. In 1989 she formed her company, Natural Cotton Colours Inc., and now contracts production of the cotton to farmers in Arizona and Texas. She designs fabrics with her cotton and has received international recognition for the development of Fox Fiber. 1.31

Adriana Franco was born in Argentina in 1957. She studied Clinical Psychology in Buenos Aires, moving to the USA to train in Environmental Perceptive Issues at Harvard University, and Environmental Planning and Design at Massachusetts Institute of Art. Her professional career started in 1982 in Paris, where she worked as a colourist for the French Ministry of Urban Planning. On her return to Buenos Aires she founded her own design studio, specializing in architectural colouring and interior design. She has worked on colour collections for wall-to-wall carpet manufacturers and furniture and carpet design for private clients. In 1992 she held a solo exhibition and since then has lectured at the University of Buenos Aires and conducted seminars on carpet design and the use of colour in textiles. 6.27

Susie Freeman was born in London in 1956. She took a foundation course at Manchester Polytechnic, followed by a BA in Textiles and Fashion, and later an MA in Textiles at the Royal College of Art, London. She has received recognition for her work since 1979 when she was awarded first prize for knitted fabrics at the Courtaulds/Leeds Art Gallery Textile Competition. In 1981 she was given a Setting-up Grant from the Crafts Council; in 1984 she was awarded a Churchill Memorial Travelling Fellowship to India; and in 1988 she received a Crafts Council Research Bursary. Susie Freeman exhibits her work frequently, holding shows in London, the USA and Japan. Her most recent have been the Anniversary Show, Miharudo Gallery, Mejiro, Tokyo, in 1993; a One Person Show at Mobilia, Cambridge, Massachusetts in 1994; and 'Deckchairs', a touring exhibition for Southern Arts/Winchester Gallery, also in 1994. Since starting as a textile designer she has sold her work successfully within the UK. She has also knitted fabrics for firms such as Labyrinth, Dark Crystal and Willow. 2.1, 2

Aija Freimane studied at the Applied Art College of Riga, Latvia, and is completing a further period of study there, specializing in textile design. She teaches handicraft at the Applied Art College of Riga and is Editor of the women's needlework magazine Zeltene. 7.25, 26

Kazimiera Frymark-Blaszczyk lives and works in Lódz, Poland. She graduated from the Academy of Fine Arts and Design in 1955 with a specialization in Textile Art and Fashion Design. In 1967 she began her interest in knitting design and today is the Head of a department specializing in the craft at Lódz Academy. Her work encompasses woven and knitted tapestries and small format and painted works as well as manufactured lines. She has exhibited her work at solo shows in Poland, Czechoslovakia, the UK, Holland,

Denmark, Sweden and Mexico, and examples of her designs can be seen in permanent collections throughout Europe and in the USA. 3.23

Fujie Textile was established in 1885. Their interior fabrics emphasize the three main elements of design: material, colour and form. They create up-to-date products of high and reliable quality and, through extensive research of the domestic and international markets, are now supplying these throughout the world. 5.25

Anna Gerretz was born in 1959 and educated at the Tallinn Art University, Estonia. She has held solo exhibitions within Estonia and group exhibitions in Finland, Russia, Sweden, Germany, the USA and Belgium. 6.24

Romeo Gigli was born at Castelbolognese, Faenza, Italy. After classical studies at school he read architecture at university. In 1979 he moved to New York and worked in the textile studio of Dimitri before returning to Italy and opening his own workshop. Today his fashion designs are known throughout the world. 5.1

Di Gilpin established her workshop at Struan, Skye, in 1983. She is primarily a designer and sells her own knitwear and knitting kits alongside a range of yarns including Shilasdair for the Skye Yarn Company. 4.21

Clare Goddard studied sculpture at the Gerrit Rietveld Academy, Amsterdam, The Netherlands, and continued her studies at the Royal College of Art, London, where she gained an MA in Textile Design. Since 1991 she has been exhibiting her work in London and in 1994 took part in the 'Futuristic Rococo' Hat Show in Japan. She has worked as a freelance designer in Italy, Paris and New York, collaborating in the collections of Perry Ellis, Donna Karan and Kogi Tatsuno. Pages 2, 11

Margara Griffin was born in La Plata, Argentina, in 1960. She is a textile designer, having graduated from the College of Architecture, Buenos Aires University, where she now teaches. Before setting up her own studio making hand-printed tablecloths and napkins she worked for five years as a colourist. 1.3

Gudrún Gunnarsdóttir was born in Reykjavik, Iceland, and trained in Kim Naver's Studio, Copenhagen, Denmark, before completing her studies at the Haystack Mountain School of Art and Craft in Maine, USA. She has exhibited her work widely in Iceland in both solo and group shows and has work in the permanent collections of the National Gallery, Iceland, and the Reykjavik Art Museum. She has been a freelance textile designer since 1976. 4.34

Koji Hamai was born in Japan in 1964 and graduated from the Bunka Fashion College. He believes strongly in the importance of the textile in fashion design and is well known for producing highly fashionable fabrics. He initially joined Miyashin Corporation in Hachioji, where he acquired a knowledge of textile production. In 1986 he moved to the Issey Miyake Design Studio, where he stayed until 1991, leaving to work as a free-lance fashion designer. Koji Hamai has received many awards within Japan. Page 6, 1.30, 6.2

Drahomira Hampl was born in 1959 in Czechoslovakia, but now lives and works in Germany. She studied Textile Art at the College of Art in Cologne, Germany; and graduated in Textile Design from the College of Art and Design in Krefeld in 1994. Since then she has been experimenting on sample looms on the themes of fabric language and structure. 3.9, 10, 11

Tara Hansford studied at Bournemouth College of Art and Design, Dorset, and Loughborough College of Art and Design, receiving a BA Honours degree in Embroidery. In 1994 she completed an MA in Embroidered Textiles at the Royal College of Art, London, at which time she was presented with the Daler-Rowney/RCA 1994 Painting Award. She has undertaken study periods in India, where she developed embroidery designs for fashion/interior collections selling to international companies including Conran and Issey Miyake. She also worked on the Flyte/Ostell Spring/Summer 1994 collection, creating embroidery techniques for several garments which were shown in New York and London. 7.22

Jane Harris studied at the Glasgow School of Art where she received a BA Honours degree in Woven and Embroidered Textile Design. Further training followed in life drawing and photography at the Duncan of Jordanstone College of Art and Design, Dundee, and in general art and design (specializing in sculpture) at the Chelsea School of Art, London. She has been visiting lecturer at the Parsons Institute of Art and Design, New York, the Glasgow School of Art and the Decorative Arts Department of Glasgow University. In 1994 she prepared a series on the applied arts in Great Britain, a Kaleidoscope Special broadcast for Radio 4 in the UK. Jane Harris has exhibited widely in the UK, including a solo show at the Kelvingrove Museum and Art Gallery in Glasgow in 1994. In 1994 she was also awarded the Scottish Arts Council Craft Development Award. 3.3, 4, 5

Sue Hartree graduated with a BA Honours degree in Textile Design (Woven Fabrics) from the Surrey Institute of Art and Design in 1994, and is currently taking an MA there. She had held group exhibitions at the New Designers Show, London, and Texprint 1994 at Interstoff, Frankfurt, Germany. Her work can be seen in the South-East Art and Craft Collection at the Hove Museum and Art Gallery, Sussex. 7.32

Fiona Hely-Hutchinson was born in Ireland in 1965. She attended a course in Visual Education at Limerick College of Art and Design, after which she studied for a National Diploma in Textile Design in Galway which she received in 1990. Following a year's course in Business and Design she worked as a freelance designer, producing tapestries for exhibitions and to commission, before joining a rug-making factory in Roscommon where she wove sample rugs for the US market. Today she works from her home in Limerick designing and making tapestries. 7.24

Lucie Hernandez received a BA Honours degree in Fashion/Textiles from John Moores University, Liverpool. In the course of her studies she spent a period at Tuebrook Primary School in Liverpool, teaching children how to weave. Since graduation she has worked for the furniture designer Tom Dixon. She has received a commendation for a woven sample from Bradford Textile Society and has exhibited her work at the Surtex Design Show in New York. 7.19

Sylvia Heyden was born as Silvia Stucky in Basle, Switzerland, in 1927 and graduated from the School of Design, Zurich. She has held solo exhibitions in the USA, Germany and Switzerland since 1972 and her work can be seen in many permanent collections, including the North Carolina Museum of Art at Raleigh, the Mint Museum of Art at Charlotte, North Carolina, and the Williams College Museum, Williamstown, Massachusetts. 3.36

Katrin Hielle was born in 1968 and studied textile design at the Technical College in Reutlingen, Germany. She worked for six months with Création Baumann in Switzerland in 1993 before joining Rohi Stoffe GmbH. She

has recently finished a thesis on Jacquard design for aircraft. 3.26

Yoshiki Hishinuma is a fashion and textile designer who was born in Sendai, Japan, in 1958. He has presented collections since 1984, showing both in Japan and Europe. In 1992 he became the subject of a monograph, 'Here and There', and exhibited his work at EXPO '92, Seville, Spain. Since 1993 he has been costume director of Universiade '95, Fukuoka. 4.1, 4, 5

Charlotte Hodge was educated at Manchester Polytechnic, UK, where she received a BA Honours degree in Textiles/Fashion, specializing in embroidery. In 1992 she was awarded a Prince's Trust Youth Business Bursary for starting up in business. She has held solo exhibitions in the UK and received commissions from clients in the UK and Saudi Arabia. 6.18, 20

Pat Hodson studied painting at Liverpool College of Art, UK. She has exhibited widely in Britain and has taken part in shows in both China and Indonesia. Her work can be seen in public and private collections. 2.29

Zoe Hope trained at Middlesex University, UK, graduating with a first class Honours degree in Constructed Textiles. Today she specializes in making wall-hangings and smaller framed pieces commissioned by private buyers and shops such as Paperchase and Marks and Spencer in England and overseas. She also works with interior designers on specific projects; recently this has included designing and making fabric for curtains in a London home and designing a mirror frame commissioned by *Elle Decoration* for Decorex International 1994. Zoe Hope has exhibited her work within the UK and in the Permaculture Earth Paper Exhibition in Tokyo, Japan in 1995. 2.4, 5

Anne Hübel was born in 1964 in Birgsteinfurt, Germany. She studied textile design at the Textilwerke Jo Bierbalm (1984); the Webereibetrieb Wichmann (1987); the Firma Taunus Textildruck (1990) and the Firma Zangs Stickerei Krefeld (1993), specializing in screen printing, weaving and embroidery art. She has recently completed a Diploma in Textile Design at the University of Kassel Menzelstrasse and showed the resultant embroidery in the exhibition 'Stretch under Stress' (1994). 7.31

Jackytex, founded in 1972, supplies knitted fabric to designers worldwide. The typical Jackytex product is cut knitwear using yarns and Jacquard techniques. However, due to the demand for tailoring, the PLAIN line was also created in 1982, offering a range of plain fabrics for T-shirts, suits and coats. 4.3

Dorte Østergaard Jakobsen was born in Denmark in 1957 and studied at the College of Arts and Crafts, Copenhagen in 1984. After graduation he was a member of the textile group Emballage for two years before spending 12 months in Italy teaching at the Politecnico di Milano. Today he is a partner in the textile and furniture group Alivedesign, along with the industrial designer Jakob Berg. Dorte Østergaard Jakobsen frequently exhibits his work in Denmark and has also shown in Sweden, Germany and Italy. 1.19, 20

Feliksas Jakubauskas was born in Lithuania in 1949. He graduated in 1964 from the Kaunas Junior School of Applied Arts, having studied interior design. From 1974–6 he attended the Lithuanian Academy of Arts in Vilnius and from 1976–80 trained in the tapestry department of the Academy of Applied Arts in Budapest, Hungary. He has held solo exhibitions in his native country and Norway and taken part in exhibitions throughout the world, most recently at the International Textile Exhibition, 'Visions-Convergence' in 1994 in Minneapolis, USA, and 'Graz ITS' in Graz, Austria, also in 1994. His work can be seen in museum collections in Vilnius. 2.6, 4.11, 6.25

Marija Jenko (see Almira Sadar)

Tania Johnson studied Fashion/Textiles and Business Studies at Brighton University, receiving a BA Honours degree with a specialization in woven textiles. She has exhibited her fabrics at the New Designers Show, London. She is currently studying woven textiles at the Royal College of Art, London. 7.20

Hella Jongerius was born in 1963 and attended the Academie Industriele Vormgeving in Eindhoven, The Netherlands. She has exhibited at Le Vent du Nord in Paris and at Droog Design in Milan. 3.22

Bodil Kellermann was born in Aarhus, Denmark, in 1951. She attended the Skals School of Handcrafts and later studied weaving at the Regitze Valentiner and Charlotte Schröder School in Copenhagen, and interior design at the Aarhus Architecture School. Since graduating she has worked for Lis Ahlman and Kvadrat. 4.28

Beppe Kessler studied at the Gerrit Rietveld Academy, Amsterdam, The Netherlands, in 1979 and today is designer for Taunus Textildruck and a teacher at the Minerva Art Academy in Groningen. She exhibits her work in The Netherlands. 6.1

Louise Kilner studied at the Surrey Institute of Art and Design and is currently working for an MA degree in Textiles and Fashion at the University of Central England, specializing in the layering of printed textiles. In 1994 she was selected for the International Textile Design Contest at The Space, Omotesando, Tokyo and also as a potential 'Distinction' Licentiate with the Society of Designer-Craftsmen. 7.9

Knoll Group is a global manufacturer of office furnishings, including contract textiles. It was founded in 1938 by Hans G. Knoll with his wife, Florence Knoll, an architect and designer. Today Knoll have offices throughout North America, Europe, Latin America and Asia. 4.29

Ieva Krumina was born in Riga, Latvia, in 1964. In 1983 she graduated from the Riga Applied Arts School and in 1989 from the Department of Textile Art at the Latvian Academy of Arts. Since then she has been a member of the Young Artists' Union. She has participated in textile shows in Latvia, Australia, Austria, Denmark and Germany and at present teaches at the Latvian Academy of Arts. In 1993 she received a Master's degree in Fine Arts. 6.6, 7

Robert Lamarre was born in Montreal, Canada, in 1950. He studied exhibition design at the Institut des Arts Appliqués in Montreal and graphic design at the Université du Quebec before taking a teaching Diploma. In 1986 he spent some time in England researching computer-aided textile design at Goldsmiths' College, London, and conducting a survey of the art and design education system in Great Britain. He holds many professional memberships in Canada including the Association des Designers Textiles du Quebec, which he founded in 1991. Robert Lamarre is a well-known figure on the teaching circuit in Canada, frequently giving papers and holding conferences. In 1985 he co-founded the Centre de recherche et de design en impression textile de Montréal with Monique Beauregard. Most recent exhibitions include a group show at the Galerie Marouska, Lyons, France in 1993, and 'Skin and Bones' in Toronto in 1994. 2.25

Eva Fleg Lambert learned weaving and spinning skills while living in Turkey and later in Greece. In 1971 she set up her own studio on the Isle of Skye, where she specialized in producing floor and tapestry-woven rugs. She has developed her own yarn, marketed through her company Shilasdair, using a flock of coloured sheep. The business has expanded by using hand-selected sheep from Skye and the mainland and she enhances the colour of the fleece with selected natural dyes. 4.20

Nina Laptchik graduated from the L'viv State Institute of Decorative and Applied Arts in the Ukraine in 1983. She has held solo exhibitions in the Ukraine and France, and her work has been selected for group shows in Denmark, Hungary and Russia. She exhibited in Belgium at the 1993 Contemporary Tapestry-Cloth Arts exhibition which had as its theme 'The Other Europe'. 5.20

Jack Lenor Larsen was born in 1927 in Seattle, Washington. He studied architecture, furniture design and weaving at the University of Washington and elsewhere, and opened a weaving studio in 1949. He completed an MFA at Cranbrook Academy of Art, Michigan, in 1951, moved his studio to New York and in 1953 founded the firm which today carries his name in the international market. In 1958 the Larsen Design Studio was founded, and expansion began in 1968 with the opening of JLL International offices in Zurich, Paris and Stuttgart; carpet, leather and furniture divisions were created between 1973 and 1976. Larsen has been Artist in Residence at the Royal College of Art, London, and curator of 'Wall-hangings' at the Museum of Modern Art, New York. From 1981-9 he was President of the American Craft Council, becoming President Emeritus in 1990. In 1992 he founded the LongHouse Foundation in East Hampton, New York. Jack Lenor Larson is affiliated to most of the leading US design institutions, including the American Institute of Architects and the American Society of Interior Designers. His work can be seen in the permanent collections of leading design museums throughout the world. In 1993 he was awarded the Brooklyn Museum Design award for Lifetime Achievement. 4.14

Juha Laurikainen was born in Finland in 1955 and today lives and works in Hämeenlinna as a teacher of design at the Häime Polytechnic/Wetterhoff Institute of Crafts. She studied at the University of Industrial Arts and at the Ecole Supérieure des Arts Visuels de la Cambre in Brussels, Belgium. She has designed printed fabrics for Marimekko, Finlayson and Helenius, and woven fabrics for Wetterhoff. From 1991-2 Juha Laurikainen was the Vice President of TEXO. 4.27

Christopher Leitch is a textile designer who lives and works in Kansas City, USA. He has designed costumes for many private collections and public productions, notably for the Spanish Surrealist playwright Fernando Arabal's production of 'and they put handcuffs on the flowers'. Leitch took a BFA at Kansas City Art Institute and studied for an MA in Visual Arts from Goddard College, Vermont. With Stephanie Nuria Sabato he founded Ganga. He is curator of the exhibition 'Crossing Borders–Contemporary Australian Textile Art', touring the USA for two years from 1995. 1.1, 2, 6

Christianna Los studied Fine Art at the Byam Shaw School of Drawing and Painting, London. Before undertaking a postgraduate course in textiles at Goldsmiths' College, specializing in tapestry weaving, she designed and sold knitwear in Scotland. Since 1988 she has exhibited in Britain and has worked on commissions for private clients in the south of France and Monaco. She is an active member of a national exhibiting group, New Fibre Art, and of the Society of Designer-Craftsmen. 1.12, 13

Tom Lundberg was educated at Iowa State University, USA, from 1971-5, receiving a BFA degree with Special Honours and Distinction in Painting and a Teacher's Certification for Art. Further training followed at Indiana State University where he graduated with an MFA in 1979. At present he is Professor at Colorado State University and a leading figure in the fibre arts world, lecturing regularly at leading universities and colleges in the USA. He has exhibited his work both nationally and internationally including the Craft Today USA touring show which visited twelve countries from 1989-92. He has received many awards, including an Excellence Merit in the Fiber/Texture show in 1993 at the Boulder Art Center, Colorado. Lundberg's designs can be seen in the permanent collections of the American Craft Museum, New York, the Indianapolis Museum of Art, and the Chase Manhattan Bank, New York. In 1994 he was a Juror at Fiberworks '94, Oklahoma City, and a panellist at 'Textiles about Textiles' at the Textile Museum, Washington DC. 6.14

Vallerie Maden studied Creative Embroidery at the City and Guilds College, London. She already had a working background of silversmithing, silk-screen printing, batik, weaving and dyeing. She is a member of the Cheshire Textile Group and a Full Member of the Embroiderers' Guild. As well as teaching papermaking and feltmaking in various schools she lectures in Textile Art at the Bury Arts and Crafts Centre, Lancashire. 1.29

Chiaki and **Kaori Maki** studied at the Musashino Art University, Tokyo and the Rhode Island School of Design, USA. She worked for Toray Co. and Pashu Co. in Tokyo before founding the Maki Textile Studio in 1990. The studio uses Asian natural materials to create contemporary textiles, employing unique methods, and is currently working with the designer Neeru Kumar. In 1992 Kaori Maki, Chiaki's younger sister, joined the company. Kaori, also a graduate of the Rhode Island School of Design, worked for a period with Jack Lenor Larsen, then returned to Kyoto to work as a designer for the Kawashima Textile Company. The work of the Maki sisters has received international acclaim and can be found in the permanent collections of the Saint Louis Art Museum and the Minneapolis Institute of Arts in the USA. 4.15-19

Peter Maly, a furniture, textile and interior designer, trained at the Detmold School of Architecture, Germany, after which he became an editorial adviser to the German magazine *Schöner Wohnen*. In 1970 he set up his own studio in Hamburg. He has designed products that have been manufactured by some of the best-known German furniture manufacturers, including Reim Interline and Walter Knoll. 3.24

Elisabeth Mann was born in Vienna, Austria, and raised in Nottingham, England. She started her professional career as a social worker, but later studied textile design and today is a freelance tutor of decorative paint techniques and textiles for interiors. Her work mainly consists in creating cushions, curtains, throws and screens and she works to commission and exhibits throughout England. She is a Licentiate Member of the Guild of Designer-Craftsmen. 5.10, 11

Patrizia Marcato is designer Luciano Marcato's daughter. She graduated in design in London and since 1982 has worked for her family firm as stylistic-creative manager. 5.7

Rizijs Marians is a third-year student at the Latvian Academy of Art. 7.10

Marieta Textiles, founded in 1974 by Maria Cardoner, is a small textile company dedicated to the printing and marketing of upholstery fabrics designed by avant-garde pictorial artists such as Xavier Mariscal, Silvia Gubern, Maarten Vrolijk, Xano Armenter, Phillip Stanton and Regina Saura. Examples of Marieta's designs can be found in the Philadelphia Museum of Arts, USA; the Kunst Museum,

Düsseldorf, Germany; and the Fond National d'Art Contemporain, Paris, France. 5.2, 22

Martin McShane trained in catering before switching to fashion textiles, which he studied at Loughborough College of Art and Design, taking a BA Honours degree in Multimedia Textiles, and the RCA, where he is currently working for an MA in Embroidery. From 1993–4 he worked for Nigel Atkinson Textiles producing fabrics for interiors, and exclusive fabrics and accessories for fashion houses. He has exhibited at the New Designers Show, London, the Loughborough Tactile Textile Show, London, and the Knitting and Stitching Show, London and Harrogate. 7.18

Kurt Meinecke is the founder and creative principal of the US corporate identity design firm Group/Chicago (founded in 1980). He is a painter and sculptor whose works have been exhibited internationally and is also the creator of a line of home furnishing products for the interior design market. Kurt Meinecke's graphic design work has been honoured with awards from the New York Art Director's Club, Graphic, Communication Arts, the American Institute of Graphic Arts, *Print* magazine and the American Centre for Design. He is a graduate of Washington University School of Fine Arts and a current member of the 27 Chicago Designers.

Missakian/Contarsy Design Team was founded by Anais Missakian and Elise Contarsy. Both women are graduates of the Rhode Island School of Design, USA, and are specialists in the field of decorative home textiles. They design collections for textile manufacturers in the USA, Europe and Asia. Elise Contarsy has been an instructor of textile design at the Parsons School of Design, and Anais Missakian is a full-time faculty member in the Textile Department of the Rhode Island School of Design.

Eiji Miyamoto was born in the textile manufacturing city of Hachioji, Japan, in 1948, graduating from Hosei University, Tokyo, in 1970. He joined his father's textile firm, Miyashin Co. Ltd, and is today the Managing Director. In 1988 he joined the Hachioji Fashion Team. He has exhibited his designs within Japan and lectures at the Bunka Fashion College. 3.13, 15, 16

Anne Fabricius Møller was born in 1959 and trained in the Textile Department of the College of Arts and Crafts, Copenhagen. She now works as a freelance textile designer at the fashion company In-Wear A/S. She has shown her work at various venues within Denmark and in 1991 was awarded the Copenhagen Polytechnic Art and Craft Prize of 1879. She is a member of OCTO. 1.32, 4.39, 40

Tina Moor was born in Küsnacht, Zurich, Switzerland, and attended art school there. In 1987 she won a textile scholarship to train at the Schoeller Hardturn, Zurich, and from 1988–93 took classes and received practical training at Création Baumann, Langenthal, with the designer Karl Höing in Italy and at the Taunus Textildruck in Frankfurt, Germany. Since 1993 she has run her own studio for weaving design in Zurich, together with Simone Tremp and Ursula Schultheiss. 3.1, 6

Ulf Moritz was born in Germany in 1939 and qualified as a textile designer at Textilingenieurschule, Krefeld, in 1960. He worked for Weverij de Ploeg before setting up his own design studio in 1970. Since then he has been designing furnishings for Sahco Hesslein and Interlübke, carpets for MID, Oliver Treutlein and Reim Interline, and furniture for Reim Interline and Montis. He launched his own fabric collection, Ulf Moritz by Sahco Hesslein, in 1986 and his own carpet collection, Ulf Moritz by Reim Interline, in 1988. His work has been exhibited in the Stedelijk Museum, Amsterdam, the Cooper-Hewitt Museum, New York, and the Textile Museum, Tilburg. Since 1971 he has been a Professor of the Academy of Industrial Design in Eindhoven, The Netherlands, and in 1992 he received the Kho Liang Ie prize for industrial design. 2.16, 17, 4.35

Anne Morrell was born in India in 1939. She studied at Goldsmiths' College, London, and the NDD Bradford Regional College of Art, Yorkshire. She recently retired as Professor of Textiles/Fashion at Manchester Metropolitan University and is a freelance embroiderer and lecturer. She sits on several examining boards and committees and her general research interests include historic textiles with ethnic work, particularly of the Indian sub-continent. Anne Morrell has written several books, most recently *Contemporary Embroidery: Exciting and Innovative Textile Art* (1994). She has undertaken many lectures in the UK and abroad, including tours in Hungary and Russia (1994) and regularly holds workshops in the UK. Her exhibitions include 'White Nights', St Petersburg, Russia, and 'What is Embroidery?', at The Whitworth Art Gallery, Manchester, both in 1994. She is actively involved in the European Textile Network. 1.22, 24

Rachel-Ann Muncaster received a BA Honours degree in Textile Design from Buckinghamshire College, High Wycombe, and is currently studying for an MA degree in Textile Design at Nottingham Trent University. She exhibited at the New Designers Show, London, in 1994. 7.13

Dora Yarid Murcia was born in Bogotá, Colombia, in 1970. She studied textiles at the Universidad de Los Andes in Bogotá. In 1994 she presented her experimental fibre Calotropis at two major design fairs in Colombia. 4.26

Jill Myerscough was born in Bristol, UK, in 1948. Following a drawing course and a Diploma in Art and Design from Trowbridge College, Wiltshire, she studied for a BA Honours degree in Textile/Fashion Design at Winchester School of Art, graduating in 1994. She has exhibited at local galleries and at the Knitting and Stitching Show, London, 1994. 7.6

Jette Nevers was born in Denmark in 1943 and graduated from Kolding Kunsthandvaekerskole in 1965. Since then he has owned his own weaving workshop. He has frequently shown his work within Denmark and has also exhibited in the USA and Japan. 2.15

Adriane Nicolaisen studied anthropology at UC Berkeley, California, graduating with a BA degree in 1972. Further periods of study followed throughout the 1970s and 1980s at both the Mendocino Art Centre and Berkeley. Adriane Nicolaisen is the founder of Handwoven Webworks which has produced original handwoven fabrics since 1987. She has exhibited her work at the American Crafts Council in Baltimore and San Francisco each year since 1991. Other recent shows include 'Adriane Nicolaisen Handwovens and Mark Sutton Jewellery' at the Mind's Eye in Scottscale, Arizona (1994) and the Flying Shuttle in Seattle, Washington, also in 1994. Adriane has taught textile design at the Mendocino Art Centre, where she was Artist in Residence in 1990, and at the College of the Redwoods, Fort Bragg. 4.36

Kirsten Nissen was born in Denmark in 1957. She served apprenticeships with weavers in Denmark before studying Textile Design at the College of Arts and Crafts, Copenhagen. Major exhibitions include a solo show at the Danish Museum of Decorative Art to mark the presentation of the Hofjuvelerer Poul Michelsens Jubilaeumslegat, which she received in 1990, and the OCTO Exhibition in 1994. 1.33, 34

Annette Nix trained at Central Saint Martin's, London. She has often exhibited her wool handtufted rugs and wall-hangings in the UK, and has held shows in Germany, USA, Japan, Belgium and Hong Kong. Recent commissions include designs for The Big Breakfast television show, Imagination Ligne Roset, The Royal Academy of Arts and Wolff Olins. 1.18

Maria Osadchaya and **Anna Tchernetskaya** were born in 1961 and 1958 respectively and graduated from Kharkov's Art and Industry Institute, Ukraine, in 1984. They are currently working as decorative and applied art designers and have exhibited their work in the Ukraine, Russia and Belgium. 5.14, 15

Osborne & Little was founded in 1968 by Peter Osborne and Antony Little as a hand printed wallpaper company, which expanded to include fabrics a few years later. Inspiration for their designs comes from archival material, nature and all forms of art, gardens, heraldry, Indian and Oriental traditions as well as children's themes. Osborne & Little often work with natural fibres and materials. The wallpaper collection is printed in their own factory. Osborne & Little's designs can be seen in the permanent collections of various international museums, including the Victoria & Albert in London, the Cooper-Hewitt in New York and the Chicago Institute of Art. 5.6

Diann Parrott studied at the University of Minnesota, USA, and has received recognition within the USA for her kinetic prints. In 1993 the Surface Design Association presented her with its Excellence Award. 2.14

Irene Paskvalic was born in 1964 in Brochenzell, Germany. She studied product and textile design at the Gesamthochschule in Kassel, graduating in 1993. She has received recognition within Germany and in 1994 was awarded a Commendation at the Bayerische Staatspreis für Nachwuchs-Designer. 2.20, 21, 3.17–19, 4.7, 8

Sophie Pattinson graduated from Kidderminster College, Hereford and Worcester, in 1985 with a first class Honours degree in Textile Design. Her unique style of weaving with strips of painted wood, wool and linen is a technique she has developed after much experimentation. The end result is a colourful work of art which has the qualities of both tapestry and painting. Sophie Pattinson has exhibited her work in the UK, Germany and Japan and has many corporate clients including Volvo UK, Shell Oil and Mercury Telecommunications plc. 6.10

Pausa AG is a medium-sized company located in South Germany and founded over 80 years ago. Their products are printed and plain furnishing fabrics for all types of decorations, including upholstery. 5.27

Rachel Pearson recently completed a BA Honours degree in Printed and Knitted Textile Design at Glasgow School of Art. 7.30

Glenn Peckman has been designing textiles for home furnishing and contract firms for the past fifteen years. With studios in both San Francisco and Italy he travels worldwide seeking inspiration from various cultures. His designs have been produced by manufacturers in Germany, France, Italy, India and the USA and are in the collections of various US museums. His work has recently been featured in the new American Cultural Institute in Paris, France. 5.21

Karol Pichler was born in Bratislava, Czechoslovakia, in 1957. He studied at the Ethnographic Institute in Bratislava and at the Academy of Applied Arts in Budapest, Hungary. Since 1986 he has taught at the Secondary School for Applied Arts in Bratislava as well as working for Artest in Switzerland and Création Baumann, Italy. He has exhibited in Europe, notably at the International Design Competition in Stuttgart in

1988 and the 2nd International Triennale of Art Pattern, Budapest. In 1993 he was awarded the Swiss Design Prize in Solothurn, Switzerland. 3.32

Ray Pierotti was educated in the Far East, Europe and the USA with degrees in philosophy, music, history and composition. He has held academic appointments in the USA in the Department of Languages at the University of Utah; in Graphic Design at New York School of Visual Arts; in the Department of Art and Architecture at the University of Tennessee; in the Department of Art, Theatre and Music at St Clair County Community College; and the Department of Art at the University of Alaska. He has also held numerous administrative directorships, including acting directorship and consultancy at the Atlanta International Museum of Art and Design. Pierotti has served as Juror for over sixty state, regional and national competitions and organized 45 exhibitions. His own work is found in over 120 corporate, public and private collections and he has frequently shown his designs in both solo and group exhibitions in the USA. Since 1991 he has conducted workshops and given lectures on his multi-media technique. 2.13

Achille Pinto's studio was founded in 1933 as a simple silk-weaving factory and today is a well-established industrial concern specializing in weaves, prints and dyeing. Among the company's latest business endeavours is a partnership with Toray and Mitsui in Japan and a new company, Cabeco. 4.9

Teresa Pla studied Fine Art and Interior Design in Barcelona before undertaking various textile courses in her native Spain in Barcelona, and in France, Belgium, England and New Zealand. She has exhibited internationally, holding solo shows in Spain and New Zealand and travelling exhibitions in Germany and Spain. She was awarded the Premio de Diseño Objeto Regalo in Expohogar for her transparent mask designs and has had work published in various Spanish design magazines as well as *Crafts* magazine, New Zealand, and *Threads* magazine, USA. Page 7, 2.7, 6.15

Jane Poulton studied textiles at Manchester Polytechnic, UK, receiving a BA degree in 1985 and an MA in 1986. She now exhibits widely both in the UK and abroad, including frequent shows in Japan. Her work can be found in many private and public collections, including that of the Embroiderers' Guild and the Victoria & Albert Museum, London. 1.4

Carolyn Quartermaine was born in 1959 and educated in England and France, taking a BA Honours degree in Fine Art at Cheltenham College of Art, Gloucestershire, and an MA in Textile Design from the Royal College of Art, London. She has exhibited her designs in London, Barcelona, Hong Kong and the USA and has produced collections for 20th Century Masters, Donna Karan, Signature Scarves and, under her own name, for Resort 93 and Spring and Summer 93. She has lectured at numerous colleges in the UK as well as at the Victoria & Albert Museum, London. Clients include Isometrix, Joseph, Kenzo, Ralph Lauren and Wolff Olins. 5.5

Nahid Rahman trained at the Nottingham Trent University, where he specialized in printed textiles. He worked for various fashion companies including Timney-Fowler before setting up his own company, Modern Primitives, in 1993. Today he is a visiting lecturer at Nottingham University and at Loughborough College of Art and Design. He has shown his work in group exhibitions in the UK, Belgium and New York, and in 1994 was presented with the Gold Medal at the Fashion and Accessories Awards. 4.33

Ramm, Son and Crocker was founded in 1891 by Charles Ramm who had previously been in partnership with Benjamin Warner (later Warner & Sons). The company specialized in chintzes using documentary sources from both East and West. Today they specialize in traditional floral printed fabrics as well as wallpaper, dobby-weaves, velvets and damasks. The majority of the designs are by Philip Jacobs and are inspired by 19th-century English and French documents from the company's archives, especially original patterns from the 19th-century English textile company Thomas Clarkson & Co., and the designer Jean Ulric Tournier. Ramm, Son and Crocker supply not only their own outlets in the UK and USA but in Europe also represent a number of top US companies such as Brunschwig & Fils, Lee Jofa and Rose Cumming Chintzes. 5.17

Ann Richards was born in 1947. She worked for several years as a biologist before training in woven textiles at the Surrey Institute of Art and Design, UK. She has exhibited her work in the UK and Japan, including the International Textile Fair, Kyoto, in 1989, and at the Royal Festival Hall, London, in 1990, as well as participating in a two-person show at the Crafts Council Shop at the Victoria & Albert Museum, London, in 1994. Her work can also be seen in the permanent collections of the Fashion Foundation, Tokyo, and the Crafts Council, London. Ann Richards is mainly known for her experimental juxtapositions of materials, yarn twists and weave structures to create a variety of textures and elasticity. In 1989 she was awarded first prize (the MITI award) at the International Textile Design Contest in Tokyo. 3.7, 14

Margarete Ilse Ritchie studied textile design at Swindon College, Winchester School of Art, and Surrey Institute of Art and Design. She recently completed an MA entitled 'Jacquard Handweaving in the age of CAM'. She has exhibited her work in London. 7.1

Margot Rolf was born in Amsterdam in 1940 and trained at the studio for tapestry weaving 'de Uil' in Amsterdam. From 1967-70 she studied in the weaving department of the Gerrit Rietveld Academy, followed by seminar training sessions with Jolanta Owidza and Hanna Czajkowska in Bakkeveen and with Trude Guermonprez in Bergen. She has taught at several art centres in Holland including the Rietveld Academy (1974-89). From 1973-5 she was the coordinator for the Dutch government programme in Textile Education. Margot Rolf's work has received much acclaim in Holland, and examples can be found in the permanent collections of various museums including the Nederlands Textielmuseum in Tilburg and the Van Reekum Municipal Museum in Apeldoorn. Since the early 1970s she has held many group and solo exhibitions, most recently the 'Textiel in Stedelijk Museum' at the Stedelijk Museum in Amsterdam (1993); the 'Designprijs Rotterdam 1994' at the Kunsthal, Rotterdam and 'In en uit Balans' at the Haaus Gemeentemuseum, 's-Gravenhage (1995). 3.31

Gary Rooney studied at the St Helens College of Art and Design followed by Huddersfield Polytechnic (BSc Honours degree in Textile Design) and The Royal College of Art, London (MA in knitted textiles). He is presently Research Fellow at Winchester School of Art, specializing in developing CAD knitting and constructed fabrics. He has achieved much acclaim for his work both nationally and internationally and was awarded the BUSHI Prize at the International Textile Design Competition organized by the Fashion Foundation in Japan in 1991, representing the UK in the finals. Since the early 1990s he has been involved in forecasting and fabric development for such companies as ICI Fibres, Ford Ghia SpA and Romeo Gigli. His freelance work sells to Italy, France, Germany and the USA, including designers such as Jean Paul Gaultier and

Faliero Sarti. Gary Rooney 's recent solo show was entitled 'Pleats' at the Winchester Southern Arts Gallery. 2.26, 27

Marie-Louise Rosholm graduated from the Kolding School of Crafts, Denmark, majoring in textile design. From 1986–92 she ran her own textile studio in Milan, but since 1992 has worked as a freelance designer collaborating with some of the major design firms, including Benneton (on trends, design and colour variation); DePadova (as textile consultant); Matteo Thun (designing carpets for Vorwerk) and Bassetti (designing bed linen). She teaches at the Design School, Copenhagen, and for Danish Design Education in Kolding and has taken part in exhibitions in Kyoto, Copenhagen, Tokyo and Milan. 2.18

Kristin Carlsen Rowley studied at the University of Iowa, USA, and obtained an MFA in Fibre Arts from the Rochester Institute of Technology, New York. Today he is Professor of Textile Design at the Universidad de Los Andes in Bogotá, Colombia, and owns his own company Kristin Carlsen, Artes Textiles. Before moving to Colombia he was a well-known figure in fibre arts, lecturing at various colleges throughout the USA and holding exhibitions. He was a member of the jury at the Three Rivers Arts Festival in Pittsburgh as well as at the Fiber National competition held at the Adams Memorial Gallery, Dunkirk, New York, in 1990. 4.32

Lorenzo Rubelli SpA began weaving in 1858, becoming famous for the handwoven velvets known as Soprarizzi. Today the company occupies a prominent position in the international market for fine furnishing fabrics through its blending of technique, styles and material from past and present. 5.12

Stephanie Nuria Sabato is an interdisciplinary designer and artist whose work includes graphics, packaging, pattern, exhibition, interior and fashion/jewellery design. Her work has been exhibited throughout the USA as well as in Europe and Asia. It has also appeared in several publications including *Surface Design*. Stephanie Nuria Sabato has been involved for the past thirteen years in the education of artists and designers at various universities throughout the USA and was the founding organizer of the Kansas City chapter of the American Institution of Graphic Arts (AIGA). She has lectured, travelled and lived in Europe, India and the Middle East. 1.1, 2, 6

Almira Sadar was born in Slovenj Gradec, Slovenia. In 1986 she graduated in clothing design and in 1987 in architecture.

Marija Jenko was born in 1961 in Ljubljana and graduated from the Faculty of Architecture in 1985. In 1986 she trained at the Academy of Fine Arts, Ljubljana, completing a specialization in graphics in 1990. Sadar and Jenko have worked together for several years. They have presented their experimental work in textile design at various national exhibitions, including the 12th Biennial of Industrial Design at the ICSID Congress in 1992 in Ljubljana and at the International Exhibition of Textile Art in Bratislawa in 1993, as well as internationally in Mexico in 1993 and Tournai, France, also in 1993. They both work as Teaching Assistants for Textile and Clothing Design at the University of Ljubljana. 3.21

Sanderson is a leading international brand for home furnishings. The company was founded by Arthur Sanderson in 1860 to import and distribute French hand-printed wallpapers. It expanded to include its own printed fabrics in the 1920s, and paints and bedlinens with the acquisition of Thomson Shephard and Co. carpet manufacturers, in 1975. In 1985 the company was bought by Westpoint Pepperell Inc. and extensively modernized. Recently the company has been expanding its overseas markets and operations by opening offices in New York, Paris and Toronto. It was acquired by Gamma Holding, a Dutch textile holding company, in 1989. 1.7

Louise Sass studied textiles in Copenhagen, Denmark, and Cape Town, South Africa. She graduated from the Danish Design School in 1991, receiving the Silver Medal for the Arts and Crafts Award of 1879. In 1992 she took part in the 3rd International Textile Competition in Kyoto and remained in Japan, where she worked as a designer until 1993. Today she has her own interior textile design studio in Copenhagen. 2.10

Regina Saura (see Marieta Textiles)

Cynthia Schira has a BFA from the Rhode Island School of Design and an MFA from the University of Kansas, USA. She is the recipient of two National Endowments for the Arts Craftsman's Fellowships and in 1989 was awarded an Honorary Doctorate of Fine Arts from the Rhode Island School of Design. She is presently Professor of Textile Design at the University of Kansas. Her work is represented in major public collections, including the Metropolitan Museum of Art, New York, the Renwick Gallery of the National Museum of American Art, Smithsonian Institution, Washington DC, and the Museum Bellerive, Zurich, Switzerland. Group exhibitions displaying her work include the 7th, 11th and 14th International Biennale of Tapestry, Lausanne, Switzerland, and Craft USA organized by the American Craft Museum, New York, which toured Europe for two years. 3.33

Keiko Amenomori Schmeisser graduated in Textile Design from the Academy of Fine Art, Hamburg, Germany. At present she lives and works in Canberra, Australia, where she is part-time lecturer at the Open Art Workshop and in the Outreach Department of Canberra Institute of Technology. She has exhibited her work in Australia and has many corporate and private clients, including Decca Telfunken in Hamburg and Ascraft Fabrics, Sydney, for whom she has designed her own range (Keiko). Examples of her designs can be found in the Museum for Fine and Applied Art in Hamburg. In 1994 her work was honoured with the Canberra Critics Circle Award. 1.27

Jorun Schumann was educated at the Oslo College of Drawing and Painting and the National College of Art and Design, Oslo, Norway. He also studied at the Fondatione Arte delle Seta Lisio, Florence, Italy, where he learned the technique of hand Jacquard-weaving. He has exhibited in Norway, most recently in 1994 at the Norwegian Craft Fair at the Museum of Applied Art, Bergen. Besides working in his own studio, Jorun Schumann lectures in the Textile Department of the Norwegian College of Art and Design, Oslo. 4.37, 38

Tilleke Schwarz was born in 1946 in The Netherlands. She was educated at the Academy of Arts and Industry, Enschede, where she studied general arts and textile design; and at the Free Academy for Modern Art, The Hague, taking textiles and painting. Tilleke Schwarz has held many exhibitions in her native country and throughout Europe as well as taking part in the Needle Expressions 1992 group which toured the USA. In 1993 she lectured at the Arlington Art Centre, USA, and in 1994 at the Designers/Craftsman Association, Tel Aviv, Israel. Her work has been published in various journals and publications and can be seen in the collections of the city of Amsterdam, The Hague and Zoetermeer. 6.1

Lynn Setterington was born in 1960. She studied Art and Design at York College and Textile Design at Goldsmiths' College, London. She has exhibited her work in the UK since the early 1980s, most recently at the Darlington Arts

Centre in 1994 in a show called A Sharp Local Pain, specially commissioned by the Arts Centre and reflecting the tradition of quiltmaking in the area; and also in 1994 at the Brighton and Hove Museum and Art Gallery, in an exhibition of contemporary and historical quilts, Quilts with Conviction. She is currently lecturing in Embroidery at Manchester Metropolitan University. Her work has been published in many of the leading textile magazines, including *Crafts* magazine and *Quilting Today*. 5.23

Hui Shi was born in 1955. In 1982 she graduated from the Design Department of Zhejiang Academy of Fine Arts, Hangzhou, where she is now a lecturer. She has exhibited her work in China, Switzerland, Hong Kong, Japan, Turkey, Mexico, Taiwan and, most recently, Australia (1993). She is a member of artists' associations and the Association of Folk Art Education in China, and the Institute of Art Tapestry, Varbanov. 3.27

Natalka Shimin was born in Rahiv, Carpathia, Ukraine. After finishing at art college she attended the Academie of Visual Arts in L'viv. Currently she is a member of The Way, one of the first independent art groups in the Ukraine, and with them she has exhibited her work in L'viv, Kiev, Moscow, Poland, the USA and Canada. She also held solo shows in L'viv in 1992, and Kiev in 1993/94. 5.24

Finn Sködt was born in Arhus, Denmark, and studied at the Jutland Academy of Art and the Graphic College of Denmark in Copenhagen. He has worked in Italy and the USA, as well as in his native country. His collaboration with the Danish textile company Kvadrat began in 1977. 2.24

Karen Smith studied graphic design at Blackburn College, Lancashire, before attending the University of Wolverhampton, where she took a BA Honours degree in Carpet Design and Floorcoverings. She has exhibited at the New Designers Show, London, at Interfloor '94, Birmingham, and Domotex, Hanover, Germany. 7.21

Sharon Smith has just completed a BA Honours degree in Textile Design at Nottingham Trent University and is currently working at the Jennifer Sanderson Studio. In 1994 she was selected by the Embroiderers' Guild to exhibit at the Knit and Stitch Show, London and Harrogate. 7.28, 29

Patrick Snelling became a member of the Society of Industrial Artists and Designers, London, in 1979 when he studied for a Diploma, followed by a BA Honours degree in Textile Design at Nottingham Trent University. He also holds an MA in Textiles from Manchester Metropolitan University and a Grad. Diploma in Museum Studies from the Deakin University, Melbourne, Australia. He is Senior Lecturer at the Royal Melbourne Institute of Technology, teaching design development, computer-aided textile design, textile design and printed textiles workshops. Since 1990 he has exhibited his work widely within Australia, most recently at the 4th Australian Contemporary Art Fair, Melbourne; 'Sensibilities', a solo show of interior textile fabrics and concepts, Craft Victoria Gallery; 'Crossroads' national exhibition of textile printers, Meat Market Craft Centre, Melbourne and 'Crossing Borders', an Australian/ USA touring exhibition. His work can be seen in numerous permanent collections in Australia. Patrick Snelling is a member of many professional organizations and has curated shows, most notably 'Interior Design EX' which he also designed for RMIT at the Royal Exhibition Buildings, Melbourne. 1.14

Phillip Stanton (see Marieta Textiles)

Suzin Steerman taught herself weaving techniques while at school, subsequently studying Textile Design at the Philadelphia College of Textiles and Science, during which time she also worked as sales assistant to the textile representative of Knoll Textiles. On graduation she moved to New York and worked as Assistant at DesignTex Fabrics, then became Director of Custom Development for Knoll Textiles. In 1992 she was made the Senior Designer for all product developments at Knoll Textiles. She has received gold awards for Best of Neocon in 1993 and 1994, along with recognition from the American Society of Interior Designers and the International Interior Design Association. 4.30

Anne-Marie Stewart is an artist working in patchwork and has received seven prizes at major national patchwork exhibitions. In 1991 the Quilters' Guild selected one of her designs for their National Exhibition in Bath and for a travelling exhibition to nine major venues around Britain. One of her quilts was also selected for inclusion in the 1994 American Quilters' Society exhibition in Paducah, Kentucky. 6.26

Stojanka Strugar is a Yugoslav artist who now lives and works in England. She graduated at the Academy of Applied Arts in Belgrade in 1981, since when she has had numerous exhibitions in Yugoslavia and Europe and has received many prizes for her work. 1.25, 26

Reiko Sudo was born in Ibaragi, Japan and educated at the Musashino Art College. From 1975–7 she assisted Professor Tanaka in the Textile Department. Before co-founding Nuno Corporation in 1984 she worked as a freelance textile designer and has since designed for the International Wool Secretariat, Paris, and for the clothing company Threads, in Tokyo. At present she is the Director of Nuno Corporation and a lecturer at the Musashino Art University. She has exhibited both nationally and internationally, and her work can be seen in the permanent collections of the Museum of Modern Art and the Cooper-Hewitt Museum, New York; the Museum of Art, Rhode Island School of Design; the Philadelphia Museum of Art; the Museum of Applied Arts, Helsinki, Finland; and the Montreal Museum of Decorative Arts, Canada. Page 9, 1.21, 2.28, 3.12, 4.2

Timney-Fowler was founded in 1979 by Susan Timney and Grahame Fowler, who began working together after graduation from the Royal College of Art, London. Sue Timney had studied Fine Art and Grahame Fowler specialized in Textiles and Graphics. Early links were formed with Japan, with work commissioned by Issey Miyake and Yohi Yamamoto, and the Japanese market is still a strong part of the company profile. Timney-Fowler supply specialist design consultancy services to leading fashion and household product manufacturers such as Martex, Ann Klein, Dunhill, Wedgwood, Cerutti and Etro. In 1993 they started producing their own line of interior furnishings to sell in their first London showroom. Several collections of fabrics and wallpapers are now available and their earliest design, the black and white neo-classical range, is now on show at leading museums such as the Victoria & Albert, London and the Cooper-Hewitt, New York. In the late 1980s Timney-Fowler launched their fashionwear series and today sell accessories throughout the world. 2.23, 5.3, 4

Lisbeth Tolstrup was born in Copenhagen, Denmark, in 1952. She studied literature at the University of Copenhagen, English and Fine Art/Textile Handicraft at teacher training college and from 1980–84 trained in the textile department of the College of Craft and Design, Kolding. Before establishing her own studio in 1988 with her husband Lars Pryds, a painter and graphic designer, she worked in various textile companies in Sweden and at the Trapholt Art Museum, Kolding. She has exhibited her work nationally. 6.16

Toray Industries Inc. was established in 1926 and has grown to become Japan's largest manufacturer of synthetic fibres and textiles, high-performance films and engineering plastics, as well as a producer of carbon fibre and other advanced composite materials. Toray is currently diversifying into chemicals, pharmaceutical and medical products, electronics and information-related products, housing and construction materials and engineering. In addition the company is pursuing operations in non-manufacturing sectors, such as business consultancy, computer software development, and trading. Page 11

Simone Tremp was born in Zurich, Switzerland, in 1960 and, after serving an apprenticeship as a bookseller, attended the Design School in Zurich where he studied textile design. In 1992 he opened his own textile studio. 4.10

Jessica Trotman graduated from Winchester School of Art, Hampshire, in 1992. Since then she has worked as a freelance fashion textile designer with an agent in London who sells her work on the international market. She has exhibited her work in New York and the UK. 5.16, 18

Jan Truman is a professional textile artist who studied at The Royal College of Art, London, receiving an MA in Textile Design. She has been working as a full-time designer since 1980 and now runs her own small business called Wireworks, specializing in three-dimensional structures. She is the Publicity Officer for the Textile Society and has recently held exhibitions in the UK and Japan. 2.9, 6.12

Rebecca Vaile worked as a nurse before moving into fashion/textile design. She studied at the London College of Fashion (BTec National Diploma) and Winchester School of Art (BA Honours in Textile Design with a specialization in Knitted Textiles). As a freelance designer she has sold knitted textiles to Yellow Minnow, Livingstone Studio and Prisma – L'Architecte de la Mode as well as printed textiles to J.M. Fussenegger, Textilwerke and M. Makower & Co. Ltd. She also works periodically for Holbrook and Hailey's Fashion Consultancy, London. She has exhibited her work in the UK and Germany. 7.3, 5

Joaquim Verdu was born in Barcelona, Spain, in 1948. He combined university education with five years at the Massana Fine Arts School of Barcelona, later completing a special fashion course at the International Feli Institute and a year's graduate course in finishing at the Fashion School of Milan. He served a six-month apprenticeship in a design studio in England before returning to Spain, where he worked as a designer for leading knitwear companies. He started his own collections in 1986. Since 1987 he has organized seminars and graduate courses in design schools, specializing in knitwear, and lectures at several Spanish universities. Joaquim Verdu has received considerable recognition for his work, being invited by 'Hispanic Designers' in Washington DC to present his Autumn-Winter 1991/92 Collection in company with designers Carolina Gerrera, Oscar de la Renta and Paloma Picasso. In 1992 he also signed a contract with Pullignan Internacional SA to manufacture, market and distribute the Joaquim Verdu trademark. Today his area of expertise has extended to include not only knitwear but lingerie and swimwear. 3.20

Meiny Vermaas-van der Heide was born in The Netherlands and has lived for the past seven years in Arizona. Her work is imbued with the influences of both her Dutch heritage and the colours and visual textures of the Sonoran Desert.

She has shown her work in numerous exhibitions, most notably at Needle Expressions '92, Europa Quilts '93 and Visions '94. Examples of her designs can be seen in the White House Collection, Washington DC, and the Tempe Public Library. Meiny Vermaas-van der Heide is a jury member of the Arizona Designer Craftsmen and has recently organized the travelling exhibition Focus on Quilts. 3.35

Diana von Cranach was born in 1948 and moved to Germany in 1970. She studied Egyptology, Art History and Philosophy at Heidelberg University, receiving an MA in 1975. She founded her interior design company in 1988, producing her first collection of fabrics and wallpapers, Savants I, in 1992. Since 1993 she has shown her work twice at Decorex and at other fairs in Paris, and at Heimtex in Frankfurt. She has worked on a showroom in Saudi Arabia and on the Decoration of National Exhibitions for the Krupp Stiftung in the Villa Hugel in Essen. In 1994 she launched the Savants II and Bédou collections which are based on original Etruscan tomb paintings. Page 11

Sandra von Sneiden lives and works in New South Wales, Australia. She was born in 1932 in the USA of Swedish parentage and was brought up in Sweden, where several generations of her family were weavers. In 1947 she moved to Australia and studied under the German Master Weaver, Marcella Hempel, returning briefly to Sweden to complete her education at the Mora Higher Education College. Today she is an Accredited Member of the Australian Crafts Council and has shown her work in many selected exhibitions. She is also a member of a small group of textile artists, Crossed Threads. In 1993 Sandra von Sneiden received a National Mary Durack Outback Award. 4.41

Maarten Vrolijk studied at the Akademie Industriële Vormgeving in Eindhoven, The Netherlands. His design firm specializes in tableware, tiles, textiles, furniture, paper products and a range of carpets produced under his own name (Maarten Vrolijk Editions). Clients include Rosenthal AG, Germany; Castelijn Collection, The Netherlands; and Marieta Textiles, Spain. Examples of his work can be found in the permanent collections of the Stedelijk Museum, Amsterdam; The Nederlands Textiel Museum, Tilburg; the Rijksdienst Beeldende Kunst, The Netherlands; and the Museum für Angewandte Kunst, Cologne, Germany. Maarten Vrolijk has lectured in The Netherlands and in 1993 was a member of the Jury for Mobilia Innovationprice. 1.16

Carol Westfall studied at the Rhode Island School of Design and at the Maryland Institute College of Art in the USA. She has exhibited her work in various museums throughout the USA, including the Museum of Art, Carnegie Institute, Pittsburgh; the Textile Museum, Washington; and the Baltimore Art Museum, Maryland. She is also known in Japan and India and has exhibited her work in shows in France, Mexico, Canada and Switzerland. Carol Westfall has received recognition for her work in awards such as the Artpark Residency, New York, an Indo American Fellowship and the Governor of New Jersey Purchase Award. Her designs can be seen in permanent public collections in both 5.13

Isabella Whitworth trained as a graphic designer, specializing in illustration. She worked for several years in publishing with BPC and in the toy industry with the US company MB Games as a Product Development Manager and Senior Designer. She left full-time employment in 1983 and travelled extensively in India and the Far East, where she developed her interest in textile design. Following her return she lived in a remote part of Skye and began painting directly on to silk. Since moving to Oxfordshire

in 1991 she has maintained this strong Scottish link, instigating Skye Connection, an exhibition which in 1992 presented the work of eight Skye artists at several venues in England and Scotland. Isabella Whitworth also collaborates frequently with Di Gilpin, the knitwear designer from Skye, and in 1992 was commissioned to complete five wall-hangings for the Glasgow Hilton hotel based on the legends, history and folklore of Scotland. Current work includes a series of scarves, shawls and fabric lengths as well as stick puppets. 1.11, 2.30, 6.4

Michelle Wild was born in 1966 and studied fashion and textiles at John Moores University, Liverpool. In 1990 she completed her MA degree in Woven Textiles from the Royal College of Art, London, and is currently a self-employed designer and supplier to, among others, The Conran Shop and Frank Smythson Ltd at Harvey Nichols, London. Since graduation she has been visiting lecturer at Fu Jen University, Taiwan, Nottingham and Trent University and Winchester School of Art, and currently teaches at Central Saint Martin's College of Art and Design, London. She has frequently exhibited work in London. 4.12

Hilary Windridge studied at Surrey Institute of Art and Design where she received a BA Honours degree in printed and woven textiles and dye chemistry in 1993. Since leaving college she has acquired an Italian and English agent who has sold samples of her printed textiles on the international market. She runs various practical textile workshops and has recently been awarded a Licentiateship of the Society of Designer-Craftsmen. She has exhibited her work in the United Kingdom, including at the Mall Galleries in the 1994.Society of Designer-Craftsmen Winter Exhibition. 7.14

Grethe Wittrock was born in Denmark in 1964 and was educated at the Danish Design School in the Textile Department of the Institute of Industrial Design. In 1989 she won the Kyoto International Textile Competition and studied at the Kyoto Seika University, College of Fine Art, Japan, from 1990–91. Since 1992 she has been a partner in a textile workshop in Copenhagen and recently began her co-operation with the fashion designer Ann Schmidt-Christensen, as well as working for six months for the Swiss textile firm Création Baumann. She has exhibited her work widely, most notably in the touring shows Animal-Land, Finland, and The Wild Swans, Denmark and in 1992 was awarded the Art and Craft Prize of 1879. 3.8

Helen Yardley studied at Plymouth and Manchester Polytechnics and received an MA in Textile Design from the Royal College of Art, London, in 1978. Her work has been exhibited throughout the UK and in Germany and Czechoslovakia, and her first solo exhibition was held in 1989 at the New York Furniture Fair. She has her own studio, A/Z, and many international clients including Toulemonde Bochart, France. 6.21

Wei Zhu graduated from the Fine Arts Department of the Suzhou Silk Engineering College, China. Today Zhu is a lecturer at the China National Academy of Fine Arts and is a tapestry artist at the Institute of Art Tapestry, Varbanov, China. His work has been exhibited in China, Mexico, the USA, the UK, Japan, Hong Kong and Switzerland. 2.3

● Suppliers

Helle Abild, 237 Sullivan Street, No. 3E, New York, NY 10012, USA.

Melanie Abraham, 42 Pennington Close, Colden Common, Winchester, Hampshire SO21 1UR.

Luis Omar Acosta, Steynstraat 4 Bis, Utrecht 3531 AV, The Netherlands.

Razia Ahmed, 5110 10th Avenue SW, Salmon Arm BC VIE 4MS, British Columbia, Canada.

Heather Allen, Appalachian Centre for Crafts, RT 3, Box 430, Smithville TN, 37166, USA.

Marijke Arp, p. Bedynstraat 44, Hoordwyk, 2202VK, Z-H, The Netherlands.

Benoit Arsenault, 4710 St Ambroise RM 326, Montreal H4C 267, Quebec, Canada.

Eleanor Avery, 34 Kirkby Road, Barwell, West Yorkshire LE9 8FN.

G.P. & J. Baker Ltd, PO Box 30, West End Road, High Wycombe, HP11 2OD.

Monique Beauregard, 4710 St Amboise, RM 323, Montreal H4C 2C7, Quebec, Canada.

Kristine Birzniece, 143/4 Voldemara, Riga LV 1013, Latvia. *Outlet* Dieter Wollenschlager, Kriefting Stz. 2, Bremen 28203, Germany.

Jehane Boden Spiers, 5 Windlesham Road, Brighton, East Sussex BN1 3AG.

Borås Cotton Sweden AB (Lena Cronholm), Box 52, Borås, S-501 02, Sweden. *Outlets* Australia: Borås Cotton Pty Ltd, 6.36 Boronia Street, Redfern NSW 2016. Belgium: Borås Cotton BV BA, Eiermarkt 13, B-2000 Antwerp. Denmark: Borås Cotton APS, GL Mont 12, DK-1117 Copenhagen. Finland: Borås Cotton OY, Merimiehenkatun 36, D 526, SF-00150 Helsingfors. France: Borås Cotton, Heimtextilien

GmbH, 61 rue du Cherche Mide, F-75006 Paris. Germany: Heimtextilien GmbH, Oststrasse 13, Postfach 1250, D-77672 Kehl. Holland: Borås Cotton BV, Postbus 225, NL-4940 AE Raamsdonksveer. Hong Kong: Kinsan Collection Ltd, 56 D'Aguilar Street. Iceland: Bjarni Th. Halldorsson, PO Box 1136, 15 121 Reykjavik, Iceland. Israel: Internova Ltd, 212 Dizengoff St., Tel Aviv. Italy: Rapsel SpA, Via Volta 13, I-20019 Settimo Milanese. Japan: Nichibo Company Ltd, PO Box 220 Yokohama Port, c/o Silk Centre Building, No. 1 Yamashita-cho, Naka-ku, Yokohama. New Zealand: Mokum Textiles Ltd, 11 Chesure Street, Parnell, Auckland. Norway: Borås Cotton A/S, Hvamstubben 17, N-2013 Skjetten. UK: Borås Cotton (UK) Ltd, 4A Boardman Road, Swadlincote, Derbyshire DE11 9DL. USA: Borås Cotton US Ltd, 2000 East Centre Circle, Plymouth, MN 55441.

Eta Sadar Breznik, Slovenska 9a, Ljubljana 61000, Slovenia.

Iben Brøndum, 2 Klockersvej, Gentofte 2820, Denmark.

Bozena Burgielska, 11a Sanatoryzna, Kowray 58-530, Poland.

Canet Punt SAL, c/Riera del Pinar 12, 08360 Canet de Mar, Barcelona, Spain.

Penny Carey Wells, 33 Nicholas Drive, Kingston Beach, Tasmania, Australia 7050.

Karin Carlander, 27 Solbatten, Virum 2830, Denmark.

Carpet Factory, 9 Zamkowa, Kowary 58-530, Poland.

Carrara, Via Puccini 26/40, Besana Brianza 20015, Milan, Italy. *Outlets* Benelux: Top Selection NV, Korte Gasthuisstrart 17-B, 2000 Antwerp. France: Carrara France SA, 51 rue Jean-Jacques Rousseau, 75001. Germany: Tessuti Spugna Besana GmbH, Kölnerstrasse 12-D, 40885 Ratingen 5. Spain: Besana Iberica SA, Gran Via Corts Catalanes 657, 08010 Barcelona, Spain.

Linda Chorostecki, 68 Springbank Close, Farlsey, West Yorkshire LS28 5EW.

Liza Collins, 79a Leigham Court Drive, Leigh on Sea, Essex SS9 1PT.

Brenda Connor, 13 Sevenoaks Avenue, Stockport, Manchester SK4 4AP.

Elise Contarsy/Anais Missakian, 150 Station Street, New York, NY 10002, USA.

Courtaulds, Tencel Fibres Europe, 72 Lockhurst Lane, Coventry CV6 5RZ. *Outlets* Belgium: Courtaulds Belgium NV, Ninoofsesteenweg 3, 1700 Dilbeek. France: Courtaulds Fibres SA, 20 boulevard du Parc, 92521 Neuilly Cedex. Germany: Courtaulds GmbH, Schiessstrasse 64, 40549 Düsseldorf. Italy: Courtaulds Italia Srl, Centro Commerciale Bonola, Via Cechov 48, 20151 Milan. Spain: Sointex SL, Paseo de Gracia 11, esc. C.4.4, 08007 Barcelona.

Gloria Crouse, 4325 John Luhr RD NE, Olympia, Washington 98516, USA.

Sarah Crowest, The Jam Factory, PO Box 10090, Gouger Street, Adelaide SA 5000, Australia.

Anne Crowther, 21 All Saints Road, Bradford, West Yorkshire BD7 3AY.

Dedar Srl, 35 Via Clerici, Gerenzano, 21040, Varese, Italy. *Outlets* France: EHD, 116 rue du Bac, Paris 75007. Germany: Gebrüder Weishaupl, 49 Schwanthalerstrasse, Munich 80336. The Netherlands: Diez, 7a Bredestraat, Maastricht NL-6711 HA. UK: Mary Fox Linton Ltd, 4 Newlett House, London SW8 4AS. USA: Jack Lenor Larsen, 11th Street, New York 1003-4685.

Lala de Dios, 19 Churruca, Madrid 28004, Spain.

Design House AWA (Hiroshi Awatsuji), 1-21-1 Jingumae, Shibuya-ku, 150 Tokyo, Japan.

Donghia Textiles Co. Inc., 485 Broadway, New York, NY 10013, USA. *Outlets* France: S.L. Diffusion, 23 rue de Bourgogne, 75007 Paris, France. Germany:

Donghia–Kaufeld GmbH, Grafenheider Strasse 20, 33729 Bielefeld. The Netherlands: Firma Brugman, Noordeinde 54 B 1121 AE Landsmeer. Turkey: Mosaik Design, Fenci, Kalamis, CAD No. 271, Istanbul.

Françoise Dorget, 18 rue St Marc, Paris 75002, France.

Driade SpA, 12 Via Padana Inferiore, 29012 Fossadello di Caorso, Piacenza, Italy. Outlets France: Arturo Del Punta, 7 rue Simon Le France, 75004 Paris. Germany: Stefan Müller, Bereiteranger 7, 8000 Munich 90. Japan: Ambiente International Inc., Sumitomo Semei Bldg, 3-1-30 Minami-Aoyama, Minato-ku, Tokyo. The Netherlands: Espaces and Lignes, Nassaulaan 2A, 2514 The Hague. Scandinavia: Design Distribution, Doebelnsgatan 38A 1, 11352 Stockholm, Sweden. Spain: Bd Ediciones de Diseño, 291 Mallorca, 08037 Barcelona. UK: Viaduct Furniture Ltd, Spring House, 10 Spring Place, London NW5 3BH.

Droog Design, Noordeinde 31, 2611 KE Delft, The Netherlands. Outlets Italy: Cecilia Flegenheimer, 3 Via del Pozzo Toscanelli, 20132 Milan. The Netherlands: DMD Parkweg 14, 2271 AJ Voorburg.

Johanne Ducharme, 4710 St Amboise, RM 323, Montreal H4C 2C7, Quebec, Canada.

Suzanne Duffy, 2 Laurel Bank, Geecross Hyde, Cheshire SK14 5DX.

Christie Dunning, 2443 Corona Court, La Jolla, CA 92037 California, USA.

Du Pont de Nemours International SA, 2 Chemin du Pavillon, CH-1218 Le Grand-Seconnex, Geneva.

Jilly Edwards, 99 Serpentine Road, Kendal, Cumbria LA9 3PD.

Kate Egan, The Studio, 4th Floor, 121 Princess Street, Manchester MI 7AD.

Elizabeth Ellis, 75 Church Lane, Methley, Leeds, West Yorkshire LS26 9HN.

Ingrid Enarsson, 19 Skraddarod, Garsnas 272 97, Sweden.

Ecollection Esprit, 900 Minnesota Street, San Francisco, CA 94107, USA.

Alexandra Eton, 19 Hunters Grove, Harrow, London HA3 9AB.

Fede Cheti SpA, 128 Via Gadames, Milan 20151, Italy.

Karen Ferguson, (2/R) 44 Dudley Drive, Glasgow G12 9RZ, Scotland.

Anne Field, 37 Rhodes Street, Christchurch 8001, New Zealand.

Folda Ltd, PO Box 100, Akureyri 602, Iceland. Outlets Germany: Saga Import-Export, Flensburger Strasse 20, Glücksburg, D-24960. Denmark: Wilkens Textilagentur, 9 Vongevej, Jelling, DK 7300. Sweden: Woodbury AB, 61 Axvagen, Jarfalla, S-175 44. UK: Weston Leisure, 203 Main Road, Southbourne, Hampshire PO10 8EZ. USA: Mrs Cathi Hawkins, 701 Ozem Gardener Way, Westerville, Ohio 43081.

Sally Fox, Natural Cotton Colors Inc., PO Box 66, Wickenburg, AZ 85358, USA.

Adriana Franco, 1570 Maure, Buenos Aires 1426, Argentina.

Susie Freeman, 71 Sheffield Terrace, London W8 7NB.

Aija Freimane, Mazputnini, Kauguru Pag, LV 4224, Valmieras Raj, Latvia.

Kazimiera Frymark-Blaszczyk, 63/7 Obywatelska 63 m 7, 93–558 Lodz, Poland.

Fujie Textile Co. Ltd, 4–7–12 Sendagaya, Shibuya-ku 151, Tokyo, Japan.

Ganga (Christopher Leitch/Stephanie Sabato), 317 East 43rd Street, No. 3E, Kansas City, Missouri 64111-1729, USA.

Anna Gerretz, 41 Kopli, Tallinn EE0003, Estonia.

Romeo Gigli, 9 Corso Como, Milan 20154, Italy.

Di Gilpin, Struan Craft Workshop, Struan, Isle of Skye, IV56 8FE, Scotland.

Glenanne Prints Ltd, Savile Mills, Mill Street, Dewsbury, West Yorkshire WF12 9AH.

Clare Goddard, 'Studio Seventeen', Cornwell House, 21 Clerkenwell Green, London EC1R ODP.

Margara Griffin, French 2962, 100–21, Buenos Aires 1425, BS AS, Argentina.

Gudrún Gunnarsdóttir, Oldogata 30A, Reykjavik 101, Iceland.

Koji Hamai, 303 1–15–6 Kamitemjaku, Mitaka-City 181, Tokyo, Japan.

Drahomira Hampl, Reidershofer Strasse 21, D-51570 Windeck, Germany.

Tara Hansford, 36 Mornington Road, Norwich, Norfolk NR2 3ND.

Jane Harris, 38 Cleveden Drive, Glasgow G12 ORY.

Sue Hartree, 51 Avon Castle Drive, Ringwood, Hampshire BH24 2BE.

Fiona Hely-Hutchinson, Parteen-A-Lax, Parteen, Limerick, Ireland.

Lucie Hernandez, Flat B, 418 Bethnal Green Road, London E2 ODJ.

Silvia Heyden, Rocca Mena, CH6575, San Nazzaro, Switzerland.

Katrin Hielle, 17 Schlotthauerstrasse, Munich D-81541, Bavaria 09, Germany.

Hishinuma Associates, 5–41–2 Jingumae, Shibuya-ku, Tokyo 150, Japan.

Charlotte Hodge, 5 Montacute Road, Catford, London SE6 4XL.

Pat Hodson, 26 Hartington Road, Millhouse, Sheffield, South Yorkshire S7 2LF.

Zoe Hope, Cockpit Yard Workshops, 5 Northington Street, London WC1N 2NP.

Anne Hübel, 24 Frans-Hals-Street, Kassel 34121, Hessen, Germany.

Jab Anstoetz-Teppiche, 67 Dammheidestrasse, Herford Elverdissen 32052, Germany. Outlets Austria: JAB Sales Office and Showroom, Adolf Türner/Bruno Goller, Franz-Josefs-Kai 31, 1010 Vienna. Belgium: JAB Anstoetz Sprl. BVBA, Avenue Louise 225, Boite 11, 1050 Brussels. Denmark: JAB Sales Office and Showroom, Grabrodretorv 14, 1154 Copenhagen K. France: Société des Créations JAB, 155 Bd Haussmann, 75008 Paris. Italy: Societa Creazioni JAB srl, Via Moscova 58, Largo la Foppa 1, 20121 Milan. The Netherlands: Handelsondrneming van Rije BV, Noordinde 117, 1121 AJ Landsmeer, Postbus 37, 1120 AA Landsmeer. Norway: JAB Sales Office and Showroom, Ole Reidar Hoem, Thomas Gate 4, 0270 Oslo 2. Spain: JAB Anstoetz SA, Rda. Universidad 17–Pral 1a, 08007 Barcelona. Sweden: JAB Sales Office and Showroom, Lill-Jans Plan 1, 11425 Stockholm. Switzerland: JAB Josef Anstoetz AG, Badenerstrasse 156, 8004 Zurich. UK: JAB International Furnishings Ltd, 15–19 Cavendish Place, London W1M 9DL.

Jackytex Tessuti a Maglia, Via Doggilupi 20, Oasello 25, Autosole, 52028 Terranvova, Bracciolin, Italy. Outlets Benelux: Versair Services, 12 rue Chabanais, Paris, France. Germany: Prisco GmbH, Prinzregentenplatz 23, 81675 Munich. Japan: Hamada Corp., Prosper Hiranomachi, 802-1-8 Hiranomachi 3-chome, Chuo-ku, Osaka. Korea: Dfaeyang Technoventure Inc., 16F Dukheung B/D 1328-10 Seocho-Dong, Seocho-ku, Seoul. Spain: Mauricio Morral, Rubiralta-Augusta 229 2o2o, 08021 Barcelona. UK: Misan Agencies, 2/4 Stanhope Mews West, London SW7 5RB. USA: Joanna Mandl Inc., Suite 802, 561 Seventh Avenue, New York, NY 10018.

Dorte Østergaard Jakobsen, 28 Vendsysselvej, Vanlose 2720, Denmark.

Feliksas Jakubauskas, Sv. Jene 7-2, Vilnius 200II, Lithuania.

Georg Jensen A/S, Dieselvej 1, Kolding 6000, Denmark. Outlet UK: Fabulous Damask, Signe Hostrup Petersen, Sunhurst, Crockenhill Lane, Eyensford, Kent.

Tania Johnson, 17 Celtic Close, Undy Magor, Gwent NP6 3PB, South Wales.

Josef Anstoetz Ag, Badenerstrasse 156, 8004 Zurich. UK: JAB International Furnishings Ltd, 15–19 Cavendish Place, London W1M 9DL.

Kay Tay Co. Ltd (Junichi Arai), Katsuyama 911, Fukui, Japan.

Bodil Kellermann, Norreport 91 st.tv, Aarhus C. DK-8000, Denmark.

Beppe Kessler, Burmanstraat 4, Amsterdam 1091 SJ, The Netherlands.

Louise Kilner, 18 Roman Way, Coventry, Warwickshire CV3 6RD.

Knoll Textiles (Suzin Steerman), 105 Wooster Street, New York, NY 10012, USA.

Ieva Krumina, 38 A. Deglava 53, Riga LV 1080, Latvia.

Kvadrat Boligtextiler A/S, 10 Lundbergsvej, Ebeltoft DK-8400, Denmark. Outlets Australia: Woven Image Pty Ltd, 666 Willoughby Street, Willoughby, NSW 2068. Germany: Michael Line, District 1, Forststrasse 43, DW-1000 Berlin 41. Soren Kragelund, District 2–3, Bahnhofstrasse 24,

D-2165 Bargstedt. Heinz Linz, District 4–5, Bedburger Strasse 45, D-4040 Neuss 21. Detlef Jung, Districts 7–8, Jagerhaustrasse 70, D-7100 Heilbronn. Iceland: Epal HF. Faxafen 7, IS–108 Reykjavik. Italy: Rapsel SpA, Via Alessandro Volta 13, I-20019 Settimo Milanese, Milan. Japan: Euro Design Ltd, 6F Matsuki Building; 3–8 Shiba Park, 1-chome, Minato-ku, Tokyo 105.The Netherlands: Danskina, Postbus 22620, Hettenheuvelweg 14, Amsterdam ZO. Norway: Gudbrandsdalens Uldvaretabrik AS, Postbox 38, N-2601 Lillehammer. Switzerland: Kvadrat AG, Postfach 87, CH-8370 Sirnach. UK: Kvadrat Ltd, 62 Princedale Road, London W11 4NL.

Robert Lamarre, 4710 Sreet, Ambroside RM 323, Montreal H4C 2C7, Quebec, Canada.

Eva Fleg Lambert, Carnach, Watersnish, Isle-of-Skye IV55 8GL, Scotland.

Landin Products Inc. (Kurt Meinecke), 400 W. Erie, Chicago, Illinois 60610, USA.

Nina Laptchik, 64a 29 L. Druzby Narodiv, Kiev, 252 103, Ukraine.

Jack Lenor Larsen, 41 East 11th Street, New York, NY 10003, USA. *Outlets* Argentina: Bozart Srl, Paraquay 1140, 1057 Buenos Aires. Australia: Arkitex Fabrics Pty Ltd, 162 Queen Street/PO Box 61, Woolahra, NSW 2025. Austria: Zimmer and Rohde, Schottengasse 1,3, Halbstock, 1010 Vienna 1. Bahrain: Leif Pederson Assoc., PO Box 5648 Manama. Belgium: L. Kreymborg NV, avenue Molière Laan 66, 1180 Brussels. Denmark: Atmosphere Interior Textiles of Denmark, Tjaereborgvej 39, DK–2760 Maalov. Finland: Oy Naccanil AB, Kyklanevantie 2b, pl 6, 00321 Helsinki. France: Zimmer and Rohde, Galerie Véro Dodat, 2 rue du Bouloi, 75001 Paris. Greece: Cripe, 48 P. Mela Str., Thessaloniki. Hong Kong: Altfield Interiors, 45 Graham Street. Israel: Arig Ltd, 59 Frishman Street, Tel Aviv. Italy: Concetto srl., Corso Venezia 36, 20121 Milan. Japan: Fujie Textile Co. Ltd, No. 7–12, 4 chome, Sendagaya, Shibuya-ku, Tokyo 151. Mexico: Frupo Estravagan Del Noreste SA, Pino Suaraz 753 NTE, Monterrey NL; Stravaganza, Anatole France 129 Col. Polanco, 115550 Mexico City.The Netherlands: Gerard Ernst, Weteringschans 126, 1017 XV Amsterdam. Norway: Peter Sveen A/S. Gabelsgate 8, PO Box 7561, Skillebekk, 0205 Oslo. Portugal: Casamia LDA, Rua Marechal Saldanha 378, 4100 Porto. Singapore: Aftex Fabrics, 9 Penang Road, No. 06–01 Park Mall, Singapore 0923. Spain: Pepe Arcos, Apdo. Correos No. 7, 28760 Tres Cantos, Madrid. Sweden: Hakans agentur HB, Pl 2735 Zimsdal, S-76192, Norrtalije. Switzerland: Palazzo M. Hofackerstrasse 11, Postfach 56, 8032 Zurich. UK: Zimmer and Rohde UK Ltd, 15 Chelsea Garden Market, Chelsea Harbour, London SW10 OXE.

Juha Laurikainen, 21A2 Vuurikan, Hameenlinna 13100, Finland.

Christianna Los, Red Cow Studios, Larnaca Works, Grange Walk, London SE1 3AG.

Tom Lundberg, 806 Sandy Cove Lane, Fort Collins, Colorado 80525–3383, USA.

Vallerie Maden, 8 Whitebirk Close, Greenmount, Bury, Lancashire BL8 4HE.

Maki Textile Studio, 899–7 Totohara, Itsukaichi-Machi, 190–01, Nishitama-Gun, Tokyo.

Peter Maly, 46 Oberstrasse, Hamburg 20144, Germany.

Elisabeth Mann, High Lodge, Whitleaf, Princes Risborough, HP27 OLX.

Luciano Marcato srl, Via Pacinotti, 30 Cinisello Balsamo/MI 20092 Milan, Italy. *Outlet* UK: Luciano Marcato (UK) Ltd, AB Alton Brooke, 5 Sleanford Street, London SW8 5AB.

Rizijs Marians, 86 Keldisa-8, Riga LV-1082, Latvia.

Marieta Textiles, Ballester 15, 08023 Barcelona, Spain.

Martin McShane, 7 Watermill Close, Fordhouses, Wolverhampton, West Midlands WV10 6NA.

Miyashin Co. Ltd, 582–11 Kitano-cho, Hachioji-shi, Tokyo No. 192, Japan.

Anne Fabricius Møller and **Niels Hvass**, 3 Viktoriagade, Copenhagen 1655 V, Denmark.

Tina Moor, 188 Josefstrasse, Zurich 8005, Switzerland.

Ulf Moritz, Prinsengracht 770, 1017 Amsterdam, The Netherlands.

Anne Morrell, 119 Berwick Avenue, Stockport, Cheshire SK4 3AT.

Müller Zell GmbH & Co. KG, PO Box 61, Zell D. 8665, Oberfranken, Germany.

Rachel-Ann Muncaster, 4 Wellhouse, Mirfield, West Yorkshire WF14 OAN.

Dora Yarid Murcia, Carrera 3 No. 8–13, Facathtiva, Cundinamarca, Colombia, South America.

Jill Myerscough, Heathcote House, The Green, Devizes, Wiltshire SN10 2JG.

Jette Nevers, Osterballevej 14, Otterup 5450, Denmark.

Adriane Nicolaisen, Box 1027 Mendocino, CA 95460, USA.

Kirsten Nissen, 25 Lollandsvej, Frederiksberg, DK-2000, Denmark.

Annette Nix, 24 Steward Street, London NW1 1NT.

Nuno Corporation, Axis Building 5–17–1 Roppongi, Minato-ku, Tokyo 106, Japan.

Maria Osadchaya/Anna Tchernetskaya, 128 K.95, Traktorostroitelei av, Kharkov 310 142, Ukraine/C15.

Osborne & Little, 49 Temperley Road, London SW12 8QE. *Outlets* Australia: Wardlaw (Pty) Ltd, 230-232 Auburn Road, Hawthorn, Victoria 3122. Denmark: Greengate, Ordrup Jagtvej 91, Charlottenlund, DK 2920. Finland: OY S.W. Laurilzon & Co., AB, Elimacnkatu 23, SF 00510 Helsinki. France: Osborne & Little, 4 rue des Petits Peres, 75992 Paris. Germany: Osborne & Little, Fürstenstrasse 5, 80333 Munich. Italy: Donati Remo & C. SpA, Corso Tassoni 66, 10144 Turin. Japan: Manas Trading Inc., 5F Nissan Building, 4-21 Himonya, Meguro-ku, Tokyo 152. The Netherlands: Wilhelmine Van Aerssen, Roemer Visscherstraat 48, NL 1054 EZ, Amsterdam. Norway: Poesi Interioragentur AS, Erling Skjalgssonsgt 19A, N-0267 Oslo. Spain: Casa Y Jardin, Padilla 21, 28006 Madrid. Sweden: Cadoro Agenturer AB, Nybrogatan 77, 114 40 Stockholm. USA: Osborne & Little Inc., 65 Commerce Road, Stamford, Connecticut 06902.

Diann Parrott, 875 St Clair Avenue, No. 4, St Paul, MN 55105, USA.

Irene Paskvalic, Norderstrasse 141, Hamburg 20097, Germany.

Sophie Pattinson, No 3 Sunnyside Cottages, Church Street, Ropley, Alresford, Hampshire SO24 ODP.

Pausa AG, Rich Burkhardt-Strasse 6, Mossingen 72116, Germany.

Rachel Pearson, Carriteth Cottage, Bellingham, Hexham, Northumberland NE48 2LD.

Glenn Peckman, 25 Eugenia, San Francisco 94110, California, USA.

Karol Pichler, Javorinska, 1 Javorinska, Bratislava 81103, Slovakia.

Ray Pierotti, PO Box 54385, Atlanta, GA 30308, USA.

Achille Pinto SpA, Div. – Indaco, Via Roma 9, 11040 Casnate/Como, Italy. *Outlets* UK: Foremost Textiles Ltd, Edinburgh House, 40 Great Portland Street, London W1N 5AH. USA: Joanna Mandl, Inc., 561 Seventh Avenue, Suite 802, New York, NY 10018.

Teresa Pla, 27 Portaferrissa, Barcelona 08002, Spain.

Jane Poulton, The Studio, 4th Floor, 121 Princess Street, Manchester M1 7AD.

Carolyn Quartermaine, 72 Philbeach Gardens, London SW5 9EU.

Nahid Rahman (Modern Primitives), 28 Tooting High Street, London SW17 ORG.

Ramm, Son and Crocker, Chiltern House, Knaves Beech Business Centre, Lordwater, High Wycombe, Bucks HP10 9QR. *Outlets* Austria: Perger and Sika, A-1180 Vienna. Belgium: Oasis CV, 21 Molenstraat, 8720 Wakken. Denmark: Form 4, Dampfaergevej 8, DK 2100 Copenhagen. France: Ets J. Pansu et Cie, 42 Rue du Faubourg Poissonnière, 75010 Paris. Greece: Amoreti, Theras 17, 14562 Kifisia, Athens. Italy: Mann and Rossi, Via L. Ariosto 3E, Milan 20145. The Netherlands: Hoes and deWinter BV, Postbus 1456, 5200 BM 's Hertogenbosch. Norway: Biwas, Boks 148, N-1601 Fredrickstad. Portugal: Sousa e Holstein LDA, R. Coelho Da Rocha 66-A, 1300 Lisbon. Spain: Pepe Penalver International, Valdegovia S/N, 28034 Madrid. Sweden: Tibbey and Co, Idungatan 7, S113 45 Stockholm.

Raxon Corporation, 114 East 32nd Street, New York, NY 10016, USA.

Ann Richards, 47 Preston Road, London SE19 3HG.

Margarete Ilse Ritchie, 24 Deerleap Way, New Milton, Hampshire BH25 5EU.

Rohi Stoffe GmbH, 1 Schonlinder, Geretsried, D-82538, Bavaria 09, Germany. *Outlets* Germany: Handelsagentur Pflüger, Solenanderstrasse 24, 40225 Düsseldorf. USA: Phillips Associates, 1216 38th Avenue East, Seattle, Washington 98112.

Margot Rolf, Blokmakerstraat 30, 1013 DH Amsterdam, The Netherlands.

Marie-Louise Rosholm, 15v Esromgade, Copenhagen 2200, Denmark.

Kristin Rowley, Calle 86 No. 11—37, Apt 308, Bogotá, Colombia SA, South America.

Lorenzo Rubelli SpA, 3877 San Marco, Venice 30124, Italy. *Outlets* Australia: I. Redelman and Son Pty Ltd, 19 George Street, Redfern NSW 2016, Sydney. Austria: Dkfm. M. Habsburg-Lothringen, Hintzerstrasse 9/16, A-1030 Vienna. Benelux: Ets. Georges Bourbon sprl, avenue Albert laan 169, B-1060 Brussels. Canada: Brunschwig and fils Fabrics Ltd, 320 Davenport Road, Toronto, Ontario M5R 1K6. Denmark: Form 4 Peter Robenhagen ApS, Dampfaergevej 8,5, DK 2100 Copenhagen. Finland: Oy Accenta Collection AB, Porthaninkatu 9, SF 00530 Helsinki. France: L. Rubelli sa, 11/13 rue de l'Abbaye St Germain, F-75006 Paris. Germany: Lorenzo Rubelli GmbH, Lehmkuhlstrasse 21, D-32108 Bad Salzuflen, Postfach 31–20, D-32075 Bad Salzuflen. Greece: Ependysis Ltd, 10 Haritos Street, Kolonacki, Athens 106.75. Holland: Jan de Kok Gimko Int., Smidswater 20, 2514 BW Den Haag. Hong Kong: Kinsan Collections Ltd, 56 D'Aguilar Street. Japan: Textile IIDA Co. Ltd, 1–1 Motoyoyogi, Cho Shibuya Ku, Tokyo. Malaysia: Pattern ON SDN BHD, Mail Box 56, 2nd Floor, S 11–12, Kuala Lumpur Plaza No. 179, Jalan Bukit Bintang, 55100 Kuala Lumpur. Norway: Peter Sveen A/S, Gabelsgate 8, PO Box 7561, Skillebekk, N. 0205 Oslo 2. Portugal: Pedroso Y. Osorio, rue de Gondarem 399, P 4100 Porto. Singapore: Aftex Shoppe, 19 Tanglin Road, 02–22 Tanglin Shopping Centre, Singapore 1024. Spain: Gaston Y Daniela, Hermosilla 26, E. Madrid 28001. Switzerland: Raphael Vadnai, Chemin de Rennier 2, CH-1009 Pully. UK: H.A. Percheron Ltd, 97/99 Cleveland Street, London W1P 5PN. USA: Breteuil Inc., 221 East 48th Street, New York, NY 10017.

Rudolph Inc., West Spain Street 999, Sonoma 95476, California, USA.

Almira Sadar and **Marija Jenko**, 6 Pestotnikova, Ljubljana 61210, Slovenia 51.

Sahco Hesslein, Kreuzberger Strasse, 17–19 D–90471 Nürnberg, Germany. *Outlets* Austria: Agentur Michael Alkuhn, Michael-Hainisch-Str 9, A–4040 Linz. Belgium/Luxembourg: Avenue Louise, 262 Louizalaan, B-Brussels 1050. France: 17 rue du Mail, F–75002 Paris. Italy: Via Durini 7, I–20122 Milan. Japan: Manas Trading Inc., 5F Nissan Building, 4–21 Himon-ya, Meguro-ku, J-Tokyo 152. The Netherlands: Wim Fennis, Goudwespmeent 2, NL-1218 GL Hilversum. Spain: Gaston y Daniela SA, Hermosilla 26 10, 28001 Madrid. Switzerland: Carlo Sem, Badenerstrasse 125, CH-8004 Zurich. UK: 24 Chelsea Garden Market, Chelsea Harbour, London SW10 OXE. USA: 37–20 34th Street, Long Island City, NY 11101.

Sanderson, 6 Cavendish Square, London W1M 9HA.

Louise Sass, 14Y Sundholmsvej, Copenhagen 2300, Denmark.

Regina Saura, 1 Carrer Nou, Camellera 17465, Girona, Spain.

Cynthia Schira, 1700 New Hampshire Street, Lawrence, Kansas 66044, USA.

Keiko Amenomori Schmeisser, 71 Leichardt Street, Kingston, ACT 2604, Canberra, Australia.

Jorun Schumann, 91 Kittel Nielsensv, Oslo 91, Norway.

Tilleke Schwarz, 19 Westlaan, Pünacker NL-2641 DS, The Netherlands.

Lynn Setterington, 32 Livsey Street, Levenshulme, Manchester M19 2GU.

Hui Shi, Department of Environmental Art, China Academy of Fine Arts, 218 Nanshan Road, Hangzhou 31002, Zhejiang, China.

Natalka Shimin, 109/1 Zamarstynivska, Lviv 290058, Ukraine.

Finn Sködt, 7B Skolegade, Aarhus C, 8000 Denmark.

Karen Smith, Flat 5, 348 Gillott Road, Edgbaston, Birmingham B16 ORS.

Sharon Smith, 232 North Sherwood, Nottingham NG1 4EN.

Patrick Snelling, 7 Chetwynd Street, West Melbourne VIC 3003, Australia.

Anne-Marie Stewart, 63 Belstead Road, Ipswich, Suffolk 1P2 8BD.

Stojanka Strugar, 73 Etone Avenue, London NW3 3EU.

Taunus Textildruck Zimmer GmbH and Co. KG, Zimmermihlenweg 14-18, Oberursel D61440, Germany.

Textilatelier, 188 Josefstrasse, Zurich 8005, Switzerland.

Timney-Fowler Ltd, 388 Kings Road, London SW3 5NZ. *Outlets* Finland: Nizza, Union Ikatu 45H 113C, 00170 Helsinki. France: EZ Art Studio, La Cornelia 60, Grande Corniche, 06360 EZE. Germany: Gerda Landers, Heckenroseweg 20, 22880 Wadwel; Joachim Miklitz, Uferstrasse 67, 42699 Solingen. Italy: Studio Tokyo, Piazza Garibaldi 32, 22040 Malgrate, Como. Japan: Crossworld Connections, Hills Daikanyama 1202, 1–34–15 Ebisu-Nishi, Shibuya-ku, Tokyo 150. The Netherlands: Wilhelmine Van Aersson, Roemer Visscherstraat, 1054 EZ Amsterdam. Norway: Foesi, Erlingskjalgssonsgt 19a, N-0267 Oslo. Spain: Usera Usera, Ayala 56, 28001 Madrid. Sweden: Cadoro, Nybrogatan 77, S-114 40 Stockholm. USA: Beacon Hill Showrooms, D and D Building, 979 Third Avenue, New York, NY 10022.

Lisbeth Tolstrup, 11 Asylgade, Odder, DK-8300, Denmark.

Toray Industries Inc., 3–3–3 Nakanoshima, Kita-ku 530, Osaka, Japan. *Outlets* China: Toray Industries Inc., Beijing Office, Beijing Fortune Building No. 802, 5 Dong San Huan Bei-lu, Chao Yank District, Beijing. Germany: Toray Deutschland GmbH, Friedberger Anlage 22, 60136 Frankfurt am Main 1. Hong Kong: Toray Industries (H.K.) Ltd, 3rd Floor, TAL Building, 49 Austin Road, Kowloon. Indonesia: P.T. Easterntex, 3rd Floor, Summitmas Tower, 61-62 Jalan Jenderal Sudirman, Jakarta. Italy: Toray Italia Srl, Corso XXII Marzo 4, 20135 Milan. Korea: Toray Industries Inc., Seoul Office , 7th Floor, Kolon Building, 45 Mugyo-Dong, Chung-ku, Seoul. Malaysia: Penfabric Sdn Berhad, Plot 117-119 & 200-202, Prai Free Trade Zone, 13600 Prai, PW Penang. Singapore: Toray Industries (Singapore) Pte Ltd, 65 Chulia Street, #25-01 OCBC Center, Singapore 0140. Thailand: Toray Fibers (Thailand) Ltd, 6th Floor, Bubhoijt Building, 20 North Sathorn Road, Bangrak, Bangkok 10500. UK: Toray Industries Inc. Europe Office, 3rd Floor, 7 Old Park Lane, London W1Y 4AD. USA: Toray Industries (America) Inc., 5th Floor, 600 Third Avenue, New York, NY 10016.

Toulemonde Bochart, 7 Impasse Branly, Z.I. de Villemilan F91320, Wissous, France. *Outlets* Belgium: Vanhee Agencies, Leffingestraat 60, 8400 Ostend. Germany: Design Focus, 1 Adenauer Strasse, 5042 Erfstadt. Italy:

Tisca, Via Donizetti 6, Murano 24053. Japan: Nest (Seibu), 1–18–4 Minami Ikebukuro, Toshima-ku, Tokyo 171. The Netherlands: R and G Collection, Havikskgruit 25, Zeewolde 3892. Portugal: Parisete, Av. de Paris 7a, 1000 Lisbon. Spain: Bedre, Paseo Colon 102–104 08430 Cardebeu, Barcelona.

Oliver Treutlein, Siemensring 89, D-47877 Willich, Postfach 1308, Germany. *Outlet* Germany: Harald Pflüger, Solenanderstrasse 24, D-40225, Düsseldorf.

Jessica Trotman, Flat 4, 73 Sternhold Avenue, Streatham Hill, London SW2 4PB.

Jan Truman, Wireworks, 35 The Folly, Chewton Mendip, Bath, Avon BA3 4LF.

Meiny Vermaas-van der Heide, 1219 East Jolla Drive, Tempe 85282–5513, Arizona, USA.

Diana von Cranach, Robert-Boschstrasse 6, D-50354 Hürth-Efferen, Germany.

Sandra von Sneiden, PO Box 93, Braidwood, NSW 2622, Australia.

Vorwerk and Co. Teppichwerke GmbH and Co. KG, Kuhlmannstrasse 11, D-31785 Hameln, Germany. *Outlets* Austria: Vorwerk Austria GmbH, Postfach 361, A-60901 Bregenz. Belgium: Decortex sprl, PVBA, rue Fr. Stroobantstraat 33, B-1060 Brussels. Denmark: K. E. Berggren, Refshedevej 6, St Darum, DK-6740. Finland: Travico Oy, Mantytie 23, SF-00270 Helsinki. France: Vorwerk France SA Textil, 30 Avb. Amiral Lemonnier, 78160 Marly-le-Roi. Iceland: Vidir Finnbogason hf, Grensasvegi \ 13, IS-00128 Reykjavin. Italy: Eurocarpet Snc., Via Volturno 84/86, I-24100 Brescia. The Netherlands: A. Mommersteeg BV., Dockterskampstraat 1, NL-5222 AM s'Hertogenbosch. Norway: Interioragenturer, Jan F. Sveen A/S, Prinsessealleen 2, N-0275 Oslo. Spain: Decotek, Plaza Lasala 5 Bajo, E-20003 San Sebastian. Sweden: Paul Ogeborg AB, Flygfaltsgatan 4B, S-12821 Skarpnack. Switzerland: Vorwerk Textil Schweiz, Weinbergstrasse 146, CH-8042 Zurich. UK: P.J.E. International, 41 Ledbury Road, London W11 2AA.

Maarten Vrolijk Editions, Prins Hendrikkade 162 A, Amsterdam 1011TB, The Netherlands.

Carol Westfall, 162 Whitford Avenue, Nutley, New Jersey 07110, USA.

Wetterhoff Ltd, Wetterhoffinkatu 4, Hameenlinna 13100, Finland.

Isabella Whitworth, 4 Kingfisher Close, Abingdon, Oxfordshire OX14 5NP.

Michelle Wild, 76 Kew Road, Richmond, Surrey TW9 2PQ.

Hilary Windridge, Drews Coch, Llangoed, Anglesey, Gwynedd LLS8 8NR, North Wales. *Outlets* Italy: Rowena Bristow Designs, 26 Aubert Park, Islington, London NS ITU.

Grethe Wittrock/Ann Schmidt-Christensen, Textile Design Studio, Norredbrogade 5C, Copenhagen 2200N, Denmark.

Helen Yardley, A–Z Studios, 3–5 Hardwidge Street, London SE1 35Y.

Wei Zhu, 218 Nanshan Road, Hangzhou 310002, Zhejiang, PR China.

ZSK Germany, Zangs Stickerei Krefeld, 38–40 Magdeburger Street, Krefeld 47800, NRW, Germany.

● Credits

The publisher and editor would like to thank the following photographers and copyright holders for the use of their material:

Ole Akhoj 1.32, 4.24, 39, 40. Marÿke Arp 1.33, 34, 2.22. Wayne Baillie 1.10. Jordi Belles 2.7. Sven Berggren 2.11, 18. David Bland 7.27. Mark Brookes 7.6. Iain Burgess 5.10, 11. Liza Collins 1.17. Colorado State University Photographic Services 6.14. Mike Connor 7.17. Sarah Crowest 6.5. Anne Crowther 1.23. Hector Cuinas 6.27. Steve Dalton 5.5. D. James Dee 5.13. C. Ealand 4.20. Oliver Elliott 7.12. Esprit 1.31. Robert Fells 6.1. Edward Field 4.25. Susie Freeman 2.1, 2. Yasuhide Fumoto 1.30. Mark Gatehouse 2.30, 6.4. Danny Gauthier 6.11, 7.7, 8. Rae Ann Giovanni and David Sawyer 5.1. Camilo Gomez 4.32. Len Grant 5.23. Yvonne Griss 3.1, 6. Waldemar Grzelak 5.19. Jeppe Gudmundsen-Holmgreen 3.8. Tom Haarsten 3.31.

D. Hely-Hutchinson 7.24. Poul Ib Henriksen 2.24, 4.28. Charlotte Hodge 6.18, 20. Mike Hodson 2.29. Anne Hübel 7.31. Gudmundur Imgoifsson Imynd 4.34. Tania Johnson 7.20. Felix Kalkman 2.12. Louise Kilner 7.9. Dorte Krogh 1.19, 20. Chris Los 1.12, 13. Anne Maden 1.29. John McCarthy 6.21. Sue McNab page 9, 1.21, 2.28, 3.12, 4.2. Diann Parrott 2.14. Christopher Phillips 4.3, 9. Teresa Pla page 7, 6.15. Lars Pryds 6.16. Antonio Pueche 6.19. Allen-Scott Redgrave 7.1. Ann Richards 3.7, 14. Nigel Rigden 7.32. Barbara Sachers 3.26. Mark Safron 4.36. Katsuji Sato page 6. Rudolf Schmutz 2.16, 17, 4.35. Carles Serra 6.15. Karen Smith 7.21. Sharon Smith 7.28, 29. Alan Spence Photography 1.11. Richard Stewart 6.26. Ines Tahier 1.3. Hiroshi Tamura 3.13, 15, 16. Carol J. Thorn 7.23. Simone Tremp 4.10. Meiny Vermaas-van der Heide 3.35. William Whitehurst 4.29, 30. Dora Yarid Murcia 4.26. Stephan Yates 1.22, 24.